Educational Leadership

SUNY Series, Educational Leadership

Daniel L. Duke, Editor

Educational Leadership

The Moral Art

Christopher Hodgkinson

State University of New York Press

Published by
State University of New York Press, Albany

©1991 State University of New York

All rights reserved

Printed in the United States of America

No part of this book may be used or reproduced
in any manner whatsoever without written permission
except in the case of brief quotations embodied in
critical articles and reviews.

For information, address State University of New York
Press, State University Plaza, Albany, N.Y., 12246

Production by M.R. Mulholland
Marketing by Dana E. Yanulavich

Library of Congress Cataloging in Publication Data

Hodgkinson, Christopher.
    Educational leadership : the moral art / Christopher Hodgkinson.
        p.   cm.—(SUNY series on educational leadership)
    Includes bibliographical references.
    ISBN 0-7914-0566-4 (alk. paper).—ISBN 0-7914-0567-2 (alk. paper
: pbk.)
    1. School management and organization. 2. Education—Philosophy.
3. Values. 4. Leadership. 5. Education—Aims and objectives.
I. Title. II. Series: SUNY series in educational leadership.
LB2806.H625 1991
371.2—dc20   90-36508
                                                                          CIP

10 9 8 7 6 5 4 3 2

Contents

Contents

Figures

Acknowledgments

This type of book is the resultant of many vectors, not the least of which is life experience itself. Any author of such a book finds himself standing at the nexus of a swirling melange of influences: the great writings and ideas of others, the ever-flowing interdisciplinary streams of knowledge in the humanities and social sciences, the steady output of quotidian research, the constant stimulation of colleagues and students. It is not possible to acknowledge, therefore, or to credit and thank, all those who have contributed to this present formulation of ideas. Nonetheless, I should like to express my gratitude to the following: Basil Blackwell of Oxford for permission to draw upon material from my previous works and in particular the diagram on p. 97; the Social Sciences and Humanities Research Council of Canada for generous support in funding part of this project; Corpus Christi College in Cambridge and the Matsushita School of Government and Management in Japan for providing insights into institutional ethos; and the faculty of education at the University of Victoria for its academic support.

Among individuals, I would mention the late Sir Geoffrey Vickers VC, polymath and Guardian, for his personal inspiration; Dr. Daniel L. Duke of the University of Virginia for initiating the project; Professor T. B. Greenfield for his unremitting clarity of vision at the advanced edges of organization theory; Dr. J. J. Jackson and Dr. J. Cutt, colleagues and educational leaders, for continuous moral support; and Mrs. Shirley Reeve for her painstaking efforts and patience in the preparation of the manuscript.

To the many students and practitioners of educational administration, leaders all, whose minds and experience have helped form my own I express profound indebtedness and appreciation. Let theirs be the credit and theirs the satisfaction in this evidence that the work goes on.

Foreword

The distinguishing feature of the writings of Christopher Hodgkinson is that they place administration in a clear—even painfully sharp —focus. This book continues in the path pioneered in two earlier works. And so it takes up the old themes of what constitutes justice in the ordering of human affairs and what constitutes honor in administrative action: themes that scientific management of the modern era deliberately turned its back upon. Lest any think that the errors of scientific management are buried, consider that that movement is transformed in contemporary thought and continues to flourish under the more acceptable name, management science. This is the science of measured excellence, with its obsessive fixation upon the technocratic and the spuriously rational—including the erroneously named "bottom line" and the pervasive, but speciously precise rules for effectiveness, leadership, change and implementation. The shallowness of these nostrums is revealed if one asks, "Effectiveness for what, leadership towards what, change to what good purpose, and implementation of whose values, and with what justification?"

Hodgkinson's world turns on the fundamentals of administration: the application of power, the shaping of people and organizations, the search for better values, the making of choices, and the unending quest for and questioning of the justification of the administrator's power and choices. His work lets us see the administrator and the administrative act full and fair, and often warts and all. Not infrequently the insight he affords into the heart of administration—for that is where he leads the reader—is a glimpse into the heart of darkness. It lets us see administrators and administration in agonized or repelling conditions. To read Hodgkinson is to consider questions for which there are no easy answers. To read him is to work; it is to think hard thoughts and to look at things painful to bear. The strong and the compassionate, however, will see the relevance of this work, the truth of the realities described, and their force in everyday administrative affairs. They will acknowledge the need to face these issues frankly and without sentimentality or self-deception. Although Hodgkinson does not provide recipes for success, nor yet a prescription for "effectiveness", he does show that administration can never become good in any meaningful moral sense until theorists and practitioners alike are willing to regard the depths of power-driven choice, the uncertainties inherent in them, and the ensuing responsibilities that fall upon themselves. Through his eyes, the reader sees administration in all its complexity, in its potential to thwart, injure and destroy, but ultimately—and this is the justification for the difficult journey—in its power to attain the good, to redeem, improve and fulfill.

To those who know the history and substance of science in the modern field—whose beginning is marked by the publication of Simon's *Administrative Behavior* in 1945 and by the emergence and early triumph of the "theory movement" in educational administration a decade later[1]—it is apparent that Hodgkinson offers ideas that stand in sharp contrast to the accepted professional and academic wisdom. Where the thrust of the modern field offers science and certainty—and ultimately release from responsibility through technical correctness—Hodgkinson offers choice, responsibility and the search for honor and rectitude; he offers art and morality in place of science and certainty.

His way is not for everyone. It runs profoundly against the intellectual temper of the times in administrative studies. And for this reason, some readers find his writing abstruse or perversely complex. Much of this apparent difficulty is a consequence of his reaching beyond and writing through the modern field to retrieve ancient ideas; he pierces to truths that challenge the received wisdom of the contemporary field. If there is difficulty in reading Hodgkinson, it arises from the unfamiliarity of his vision. The source of this alienation lies not in Hodgkinson, but in the contemporary field itself that happily and consciously turned its back on wisdom both ancient and modern to embrace an invention of recent times: the science of recent times: the of administration. So completely has the modern, pseudo-scientific approach—for that is what it is—denied its past that James March writing about organizations in 1965 could pronounce any idea of an origin earlier than 1950 to be "old" and largely irrelevant to the newly promulgated science.[2] Such a judgment, reflecting the now widely accepted verdict of the field, shuts out the older wisdom that is the very essence of the matters explored by Hodgkinson. In contrast to this judgment, Hodgkinson deals with the simple, central and appallingly plain Platonic questions, "Who shall rule?" and "With what justification?" It is this absence of the ancient but compelling questions in contemporary administrative thought that sets Hodgkinson's work apart. However authentically it comes finally to ring, his voice is often heard first as alien and difficult, though we may think it so only as long as we resist the fundamental questions he requires us to ask and only so long as we deny the truth of images he bids us regard.

The imaginations of those who propelled the "Theory Movement" in educational administration to its current dominant position were fired by a potent and seductive promise: the promise that rigorous theory would take the guess work out of administration and put it on a scientific foundation. Like an engineer approaching the draining of a swamp or the building of a bridge to span a river, the social scientist came to administration to set it right, to solve all its problems scientifically and rationally. It is not surprising, therefore, that after an initial resistance, administrators embraced the science, for it offered them certainty in their choices while absolving them of responsibility for those choices. Superintendent Marland, one of the early converts following the annunciation of a "science of administration," records that he "listen[ed] attentively to the counsel of social scientists." Strengthened by this radical knowledge, he came to understand the newly science-supported administrators through the metaphor of the busy pilot who

> now finds himself in the pilot's chair of a monstrous flying machine of untold power and dimensions. The social scientist tells us that there are buttons to push, levers to adjust, gauges to watch, beacons to reckon, and codes to decipher. He tells us that one cannot fly this craft by the seat of the pants, but that certain buttons and levers, when actuated, produce specific and predictable results in the performance and posture of the craft.[3]

The early joy of Superintendent Marland finds a more sophisticated and restrained expression among administrators today, but they no doubt see even more clearly the advantage of taking shelter under the certainty and authority promised by administrative science. Anyone who doubts this spirit prevails in the contemporary field need only refer to the popular text whose authors have dedicated it, in three editions over recent years, to the conviction that administrative practice in education can be "less of an art and more of a science."[4]

Not for these social scientists and administrators the observation of Blaise Pascal: "The heart has reasons, reason knows nothing of." The error most theorists make in thinking about organizations and the administration of them is to conceive them as somehow separate from life, love, sex, growth, conflict, accomplishment, decay, death and chance. The exclusion of values from administrative science, the exclusion of both the human and the humane, the exclusion of passion and conviction in all their frailty and perseverance, in all their power and

majesty does leave a residue for study—and one that is perhaps scien-
tificaly manageable. The most obvious consequence of this exclusion
leaves a field that is regrettably and unnecessarily bland and boring.
The difficult and divisive questions, the questions of purpose and morality, the questions arising from the necessary imposition of one person's will upon another, the questions that challenge the linking of
ends and means—all these matters are set aside in a search for a pallid
consensus and an illusory effectiveness. The great issues of the day in
education are similarly set aside: how big the school, who should be in
it, embracing what behaviors or convictions, reading and learning
what, using what facilities, paid for by whom, to what ends and purposes? And so many familiar, but urgent, issues are elided: busing, mul-
ticulturalism, bilingualism, streaming, equal opportunity, drugs, sexu-
ality, allegiance, community and personal morality, excellence in any
profound sense, prayer, religion, the state, and ultimately the economic
well-being and survival of the culture.

   Not that Hodgkinson addresses these issues directly or in detail,
for his purpose is to make the case that these problems are valuational,
educational and administrative, and must be approached as such.
Without applying them himself, he offers the tools by which these
problems may be addressed and resolved, as in the following propositions from an earlier work:

> The [administrator] must know two things: where the values are
> and where the power lies.
>
> The lure of efficiency leads to the fallacy of quantification. Some
> costs and some ends are non-quantifiable. True accounting is
> always incomplete.
>
> Valuation precedes rationality. One can only be rational within
> the limits set by value.
>
> First order valuation is the identification and analysis of the
> values in a case.
>
> Second order valuation is the determination of the values to be
> used in trying the case.
>
> Motives are sources of value. They may be in the dark or in the
> light. In the first case they push us and we call them drives, in the
> second they pull us and we call them reasons.[5]

   Thirty years ago Andrew Halpin warned that the social scientific
portrait of administration is egregiously, if not fatally flawed. At its
heart it is vacuous, jejune:

There is indeed something missing. The fault is that the scientist's theoretical models of administration are too rational, too tidy, too aseptic. They remind us of the photographs in magazines devoted to home decorating—glossy pictures of dramatic and pristine living room interiors.... The superintendent distrusts such tidiness in administrative theory and senses intuitively that the theoretical-analytical approach has ignored much that is reality.[6]

Such science rests on illusory and therefore dangerous images. It cleanses what is impure only by denying the impurity, the very problem to be faced and resolved.

When his novels were criticized for their portrayal of darkness and immorality in human relationships—in today's parlance they would be called "negative"—Thomas Hardy replied that "to know the best, we must first regard the worst." It is that unwillingness to look at the dark side of the human condition that prevents administrative science from dealing with the heart of administrative problems and also from ascending to the heights of human possibility and accomplishment. So Hodgkinson reminds us that values in all their possibility and accomplishment are to be contemplated and the better of them striven for. He reminds us—and requires us—to think there are choices to be made and responsibilities to be assumed.

Hodgkinson points to the errors of the putative science of administration: first that its focus of inquiry is organization theory *not* administration, *not* "administration *qua* administration"—the essence of administration, as the early proponents of the theory movement liked to put the matter. Organization theory is at best an analysis of the background factors that bear upon administrative choice, decision and responsibility. It says nothing about the choice and the decision to be made, nor the responsibility to be assumed. Secondly, Hodgkinson points out that the reason the science of administration—or of organizations—does not work is stupefyingly simple: the central problems of administrative theory are not scientific at all, but philosophical. That is, the central questions of administration deal not so much with what is, but with what ought to be; they deal with values and morality. As Hodgkinson points out, administrative science must be silent about the issues that lie at the heart of administrative action: "no science, social or physical, can tell us what is right or wrong."[7] To repair this deficiency, to regain necessary knowledge about administration, much needs doing. The task is difficult. To attempt it, some old, but underused tools turn out to be the most reliable and powerful: first, clear-eyed description, a mapping of the administrative world as it is, secondly, reflection upon that world, and finally, argument about what to do. These avenues to knowledge are restored to dialogue in the work that follows.

Hodgkinson restores a vision of administration. His title lays out the central issue. Administration is a *moral art*. He offers a vision of what administration is and of what it might become. It *is* a matter of will and power: of bending others to one's will and of being bent in turn by others. The overlap between education and administration is therefore substantial and unavoidable, if education is recognized as being the process of identifying the valuable, opening it to others and, yes, inculcating it into them. Moreover, the Hodgkinsonian vision of administration as a moral task redeems the notion of hierarchy and thereby of leadership. Everyone wants the good, at least for themselves, at best for others as well. Everyone therefore opposes evil—or what is less good—and supports the mobilization of power against it. A hierarchy of the good is therefore inevitable, as is the demand to ground it in an authority and to further it through leadership.

Hodgkinson's view of administration allows us to see in new directions, toward the world of the valuable, the right, the justified. The answers he offers are as much questions as answers. But there is a uniquely practical—or one might better say praxical quality to this work, for it considers not only the problems of administration in their general forms. He moves beyond theory into praxis, into the specific, into the politics of day-to-day living and their justification; he speaks to the mundane, but inevitable and *valuable* question of how to get through the day; ultimately he speaks also to the question of how to make one's way through a career, through a life.

There is a quality of transparency in this work. It evokes "other voices, other rooms". It leads to other realms of thought and experience. Asked what constituted the quality of great teachers, Northrop Frye replied, "They are transparent," by which he said they give access to the subject and to the writers they teach. They evoke the idea itself and the person who advances it. The novelist, Margaret Atwood, recalls what happened as Frye taught, the power of his words, his vision: "He said, 'Let there be Milton, and there was Milton'." Hodgkinson's work too has this quality of greatness in its power to evoke greatness. When an interviewer nagged Frye to square his observation of the transparency of the teacher with the conventional view that great teachers are remembered as "personalities," Frye pointed out it is the denial of ego that creates the true and memorable personality. This theme runs also though the Hodgkinsonian vision of the nature of administration and of the great administrator. "Desire," he observes, "is satisfied by *its* extinction, the desirable by *my* extinction, that is, by loss of ego in the nomothetic domain."[8] In such sharp and arresting paradoxes, he lets us hear the voices of the past, of those whose achievements bear so profoundly on a sound understanding of administration and of the dilemmas of the administrator today. Simon, Barnard, Machiavelli, Plato and the insights of the great religions are evoked through his pages. Recognizing the ancient Greek contribution to an understanding of morality in social and personal life, Erasmus, the great humanist, could pray, *"Sancte Socrate, ora pro nobis."*[9] And so may we all, recognizing in "St. Socrates, pray for us" that the problems of life, politics and administration are ancient and that human insight has already done much to see a way through them. Certainly it had done much before 1937, the arbitrary cut-off point March set as the date before which administrative science had nothing to learn from the past. Setting the clock of organization theory—the foundation of administrative science—in motion at 1937, March could call anything written before 1950 the "old" literature. Yet even this literature he considered only through the filter of "fashionableness," its acceptability to the new breed of organization theorists.[10]

Hodgkinson redresses this reckless short-sightedness. Blended now with contemporary assertion, we hear again the ancient voices and their wisdom. And much does he add to those voices: first, the foundation of value in the personal and its extension into the interests of the organization, secondly insight into how one value can be better than another and where the conflicts among them lie, and finally a vision of what constitutes right action—honor—in administration and what might make it possible to attain. Hodgkinson's enormous contributions to the field of study can be discovered by any reader willing to reflect upon the experience of administering or being administered. But to follow the way he shows requires courage and resolution—more for the wayfarer than the reader—for it entails clear-eyed observation of the realities, dilemmas, difficulties and defeats of life. Only along this path and by right action on it may a better life—and better organizations—be attained. In short, Hodgkinson is the antidote to scientism and specious science in the study of administration. His work is a gateway to the world of values—its complexities, its dilemmas, and its unrelenting challenge to attain what is good, the challenge for us to be better administrators, to do better for our ourselves and for our organizations, to make ourselves better and to strive for a better world.

—Thomas B. Greenfield

Preface

This is a book about values and the art of administration. It follows that it is also about philosophy, human nature, and the quality of life in organizations—especially educational organizations. In short, it seeks to analyze educational leadership and even to give some advice about it. Such a pretension might seem overweening were it not for the fact that there is a sort of lacuna in the literature that has to do with values. Values, morals, and ethics are the very stuff of leadership and administrative life, yet we have no comprehensive theory about them and often in the literature they receive very short shrift. One great authority, Simon, tends to discount them altogether and most textbooks on educational administration are written on the comfortable but unwarranted premise that all practitioners are honorable men. There is, then, a vacuum which this book seeks to enter, not necessarily to fill the space but to add matter where there was none before. It is written with the joint convictions that values constitute the essential problem of leadership and that the educational institution is special because it both forms and is formed by values.

But there are other reasons for the aspiring leader to study values. First, by doing so he or she* may gain self-knowledge and self-understanding. Secondly, it should lead to a better understanding of one's fellows thus enhancing the possibility of greater empathy, sympathy and compassion but also of gaining a sophisticated acceptance and recognition of the negative side of human character. Thirdly, a knowledge of value theory is necessary if we are to make progress with the problems of division, antagonism and conflict that beset organizations and societies. The leader is the one who can best perceive and best resolve value conflicts. If there are no value conflicts then there is no need for leadership.

In this book the reader will be introduced to a paradigmatic theory of value. This theory has been developed over the last twenty years and is sufficiently established in the literature to constitute a robust model which can be used for analytical purposes in the daily life of administration. The reader unschooled in philosophy should not be deterred by what might seem on occasion to be technicalities requiring previous academic training for their proper understanding. There is nothing in this exposition that cannot yield to common sense and I would urge that this section (chapter 5) not be elided or skipped since any effort expended in grasping the essential concepts should prove more than rewarding in the later praxis of leadership. Moreover, at the theoretical as well as at the practical level, the concepts dealt with here provide us with what has been essentially lacking hitherto: a common vocabulary or language about values. With the development of such a common language there is hope that some of the more forbidding and intractable problems of value may come to be clarified and made amenable to resolution or disposition.

A word about structure and style. The book proceeds through three parts (education, leadership, morality) which, though logically contingent on each other, call for different treatments both conceptually and linguistically. Furthermore, leadership is not and cannot be a science; it is a humane and practical art—perhaps the greatest of the art forms. And art proceeds always from the subjective or conceptual to the objective or real. This general line of logic or psycho-logic is perhaps reflected in the style of writing which moves in general from the theoretical to the practical, from the abstract to the concrete, and from the more formal to the more informal as the book progresses.

A final thought. This book is inevitably about wisdom. It is true that there is wisdom in the field of educational administration and that there has always been.[1] But it is an interesting peculiarity of our times that even to use the word wisdom is to risk a frisson of embarrassment. Competent, excellent, clever, shrewd, dynamic, impressive, even ambitious and aggressive—all these are commendations of the leader in the current idiom. But wise? We do not hear that epithet very often. It seems to reach a bit far. To be a throwback to the days when philosophy itself meant "the love of wisdom". Yet may we not even now argue for the ancient aphorism that to give instruction to a wise man is to make him yet wiser?

It is an aim of these pages to work against the idealistic impoverishment reflected in this linguistic imbalance and to counter the poverty of philosophy that is our current condition in educational administration. And I would end this preface with three propositions and a sentiment: The world needs education. Education needs leadership. We all need wisdom. May this book contribute, however slightly, to these ends.

—*Christopher Hodgkinson*

I
Education

Education is Special

"I am coming not to know what educational administration is and to doubt that it ought to continue an existence as an independent field of inquiry."[1] This radical statement by one of the leading authorities in the field is indicative of the very great degree of conceptual difficulty that attends any serious discussion of the topic of education and its leadership. It also highlights the confusion which can surround what to the naive onlooker might seem to be a straightforward sort of business: the operation and management of schools and colleges. After all, these institutions are very familiar. They have been around a long time, and all of us have had client experience of them at one time or another. What is the mystery? Surely their functions are well-enough understood and their workings cannot be any more complicated than, say, the running of a department store, or a small factory, or a government office?

But of course this is not the case. To argue in this way simply slurs over the inherent complexities of the concept of education itself, which, upon analysis, turns out to be one of the most complex concepts in the language. Far more complex than commerce or industry or bureaucracy. It is not merely complex but also profound. In short, education is something very special in the field of human affairs, as I shall endeavor to show.

In the first place, education is not susceptible of succinct definition in any strictly logical sense, although of course for rhetorical purposes it may be, and often is, telegraphically encapsulated. "History is a race between education and catastrophe"[2]; "Education has for its objective the formation of character."[3] Such rhetoric has its merits but it is not technically useful and, indeed, it is far easier to say what education is not than what it is. There is, for example, some general agreement that it must be distinguished from training. The acquisition of such skills as driving a motor vehicle, taking shorthand dictation, operating a lathe, cooking a dinner, controlling one's bowels, responding

to military commands, and piloting a space-orbiting satellite are important but the acquisition of these skills is not what is properly understood by education. The confusion comes about because such important training tasks can rightly be subsumed under the overall concept
of the educational project, but they are at best in the relation of part to
whole even though, at times, their pragmatic importance can deceive
us into taking them as the whole rather than the subordinate part.

It is also more or less agreed by professional educators that education does not consist primarily in the mere acquisition of knowledge,
especially factual knowledge, nor in the dissemination and absorption
of information. The operative term here is "primarily", for again it must
be conceded that the transmission of facts has a very important part to
play in the total business of education. Nor, but now there is no general
agreement, would we normally classify as education any sort of indoctrination or conditioning or programming of the learner into a set of
values or beliefs or moral codes or ethics. Yet everyone would agree
that our acquisition of values, however it occurs, is an integral part of
our education, and the teaching-learning of values is certainly somehow subsumed within the larger concept.

Without belaboring the point too much, a sense of the essential
complexity of the concept can be conveyed by the following contemporary attempt at definition:

> Education is not the art of training and subjugating people to
> serve the profit of others. It is the art of helping people to know
> themselves, to develop the resources of judgment and skills of
> learning and the sense of values needed on facing a future of un-
> predictable change, to understand the rights and responsibilities
> of adults in a democratic society and to exercise the greatest pos-
> sible degree of control over their own fate. To educate is to look for
> truth, to stir discomfort in the placid minds of the unthinking, to
> shake ideologies, disturb complacency, undermine the tyranny of
> anti-intellectual commercialism which reins in the marketplace
> and in some of our legislatures, to the disadvantage of all of us. To
> educate is to reject the false analogies of the marketplace, to see
> justice and equality as noble aims rather than as obstacles to a
> takeover bid, to insist that human progress has no bottom line.[4]

Even such an extended and deliberative attempt as this cannot,
however, be taken as generally definitive of the concept as it is presently understood in modern Western society. Many other authentic
efforts would likewise fail to capture universal agreement and would

be open to specific critiques. All of which simply shows that education is a very complex activity indeed and the fact of this complexity can be taken to have implications for educational leadership and administration.

The Evolution of Education

Educational leadership, the object of this study, is everything that consciously seeks to accomplish educational projects. But what are these projects and how do they emerge from the general or total enterprise? Is there in fact any overall project, any general purpose from which subordinate purposes can be derived? To answer such questions it is necessary to consider, however briefly, the history of the educational project within society.

This history, within Western society, is one of great antiquity. Its development has been spasmodic, moving slowly from classical times, toward rapid and exponential movements within the last century. From the perspective of our own times, it is possible to observe this evolution and discern how the cutting edge of advance shifts from one geographical locus to another. Greece endowed us with the organizational concepts of the Platonic academy and the Aristotelian lyceum, as well as the pedagogical notions of Socratic irony, the dialectic, the syllogism, and inductive and deductive reasoning; all precious ideas alive and integral to our educational culture to this day. Indeed, an historical authority as eminent as Sir Arnold Toynbee has remarked that all of European intellectual history is but a footnote to Plato. Hyperbole aside, it can nevertheless be allowed that the concept of *liberal* education, that is, the education of free men as opposed to slaves, can be traced back directly to the city states of classic Greece. Since then, of course, the concepts of slave and citizen have altered their meanings somewhat. Modern interpretations of liberation and bondage embrace such ideas as wage slavery, economic serfdom, and the totalitarian state but these, it should be noted, do not detract from the basic idea of liberal humanistic education—education which itself is liberating—an idea to which we shall return again and again. For now, let us note that education in this sense is in ultimate essence a pursuit of the verities (truth, beauty, goodness, justice, happiness, self-fulfillment) by those with the leisure or the means to do so. That is to say its aim is *aesthetic*. It could be evaluated as the grandest of human projects and aspirations or, at the other extreme, as a mere gloss upon human activity and effete dilettantism. Regardless of how it is judged, however, it is true to say that this general project remains with us still as a direct heritage from Grecian culture.

The Roman contribution to the development of educational purpose added dimensions of pragmatism and practicality. The concern of
the Romans for governance, engineering, law and administration stem-
med from imperial responsibilities and was often combined with a military proclivity for physical education. *Mens sana in corpore sano.* It is
appropriate here to note the shift from aims of liberal education toward
a more vocational emphasis. Roman education is more for the mastery
of this world than for its transcendence. A division of value appears. On
the one hand, education has terminal value; it is that which constitutes
the human *summum bonum;* it is valuable in and of itself. On the other
hand, education is instrumental, a means to an end, not an end in itself.
In this latter instrumental function it becomes the guardian of entry to
professions and occupations. It determines life chances. It sorts sheep
from goats; even Greek goats from Roman sheep.

This utilitarian shift towards *economic* purpose in education is
both ancient and interesting. The line between service and servitude is
sometimes difficult to draw. Modern technology and bureaucracy can
create their own form of bondage and a concern with pensions and job
security can be as effective a taskmaster as any plantation overseer.
Nevertheless, the economic motive is a powerful one and in this light
education is often conflated with the concept of training, a concept
which can then be rhetorically re-constituted as "vocational education". Once again, the origin of meaning can be traced historically to
beginnings in antiquity.

With the fall of Rome and the ensuing centuries in which literacy,
science and culture were under the aegis of a church struggling to
establish a new but Holy Roman Empire the educational enterprise in
the West acquired its third major dimension. This was religious indoctrination and moral conditioning. It is true that prior to the Renaissance
the cathedral, monastery and church schools of the medieval period
kept the flame of classical learning alive in Europe, but they also
invested education with ideological connotations. Education in this
sense was not primarily for work, or for aesthetic liberation, but for salvation. What could be more important, more special than this?

It is no accident, then, that a sort of moral onus clings and attaches
to the person of the educator down to the present day. And this is as
true of the Soviet Union as it is of North America, as of India, as of Africa
or Japan. The teacher is to some degree invested with a moral charge or
aura and it is this which distinguishes education from other professions and occupations. He or she is in some way an exemplar, or at least
the guardian of, a special set of values and this applies whether the
learners are graduate students in middle age and mid-career or kinder-
gartners at the beginning of their long educational journey. Whether

this moral modelling extends to educational administrators and educational organization leaders is a question important to this book and one which will be examined in depth later. For now, it need only be observed that the professions of priest and teacher are more closely related than a secular society might normally acknowledge.

By the time of the Renaissance and the discovery of America, the groundwork had been completed for the establishment of modern European culture. Greek glory and Roman grandeur had been rediscovered and revivified. The proto-scientific bases of astronomy, mathematics, and medicine had been enriched by direct Islamic contributions. The great universities—Bologna, Paris, Oxford, Cambridge—were active and growing. Learning was no longer a clerical monopoly. Vernaculars, especially Italian and English, were beginning to contest, if not displace, the hegemony of Greek, Latin and Hebrew. Europe was hastening toward the Reformation, printing, Modern German, agricultural and early industrial revolution, nation states, the settlement of other continents and the dawn of mass education. Schools now existed for others besides the clergy and the elite. Already they were avenues of upward social mobility for a few from the lower orders, a trend which was to persist and grow. Vocational training, apart from the universities, continued as a stabilizing social force through the perpetuation and modification of the apprenticeship system inherited from the medieval guilds. All of this helped in the growth and development of a bourgeoisie. The religious motive also contributed to educational growth. After the Reformation, literacy became instrumentally valuable for salvation. One had to be able to read as well as merely hear the Word and, later, for example, the Society for the Propagation of the Gospel was to take basic schooling to the far corners of Empire. Indeed the seeds were being sown for a basic conflict between the religious and the secular aims of education, a conflict of value quite apart from the already established conflict within the secular arm between liberal and vocational purposes.

These divisions became clearly evidenced in the American colonies of the British Empire. Massachusetts, for example, had had tax-supported schools as early as 1647 but they were Biblical in character and religious in primary purpose or motivation. Yet even here, sectarian quarrelling had already led towards secularism. By 1826 a law decreed: "The school committee shall never direct to be purchased or used in any of the town schools, any books which are calculated to favor the tenets of any particular sect of Christians."[5] Shortly after the American Revolution the constitution of the new republic had been amended to declare a separation between church and state[6] and by modern times these initial American moves had developed into a sharp division between state schools and state education on the one hand, and denominational schools and denominational education of whatever stripe on the other. It should also be noted that within the non-state or private sector of education a further division of aim or purpose existed between denominational and secular or non-religious schools. These divisions of law and philosophy were reinforced by the fiscal power of the state. Eventually, in the Old World as in the New, education became an arm of the state as well as of the church. Nevertheless, the U.S.A. led the way—in Canada, for example, only one Province ever had purely secular school funding and that was British Columbia from the time of Confederation until the mid 1970s. Generally, with the American exception, some mixed form of religious and state schooling persisted until the most recent times.

Many factors contributed to the steady growth of governmental intrusion into education. Imperial demands (British, French, Austro-Hungarian, Russian, Turkish, Portuguese and, latterly, American and Japanese) for political-administrative elites fostered elite systems of schooling. Industrial revolution fostered technical education and training, as did scientific progress in general. Moreover, even as the religious function of education came to be undercut, a corresponding demand for nationalistic indoctrination was a by-product of competitive nation-states in the era of imperialism. Education had both centrifugal and centripetal parts to play, both in holding together the various pastiches of Empire and in developing the counter-tendencies of movements for national and ethnic independence.

All of this may have been dimly perceptible throughout the Victorian Pax Britannica or it may have been hidden from close-up view, but in any event it was cast into sharpest relief by the apocalyptic event of the Great War. After that tragic watershed, state education ceased to be an idealistic prerogative and became instead a political imperative. The world, and education with it, had changed irrevocably.

Educational Ideals

The First World War transformed Western culture. Before that cataclysmic event there had been a culture of optimism. Europe had extended itself and its influence throughout the world, populating the empty territories of the Americas, extending imperial dominion over palm and pine elsewhere. In an ethos of progressivism, meliorism and liberalism, education tended to be seen both as a white man's burden and at the same time the key to universal harmony and prosperity for everyone—colonizer and colonized, master and servant—in the long run. After the 1914–1918 war, a war from which it can be said with some certainty that Europe, and perhaps the world, never fully recovered, the ethos changed along with the political realities. New ideologies were born: first Communism in Russia after the Bolshevik Revolution and later, partly in reaction, Fascism in Western Europe. Religious orthodoxy weakened as scientific materialism strengthened. The masses were recognized not simply as political entities but as educable, malleable entities and new techniques of propaganda were devised to serve the ends of political control and manipulation; techniques assisted by all the artifices of the new media of communication. State education was now pervasive and generally superseded older, more traditional, and private forms. Hitler Youth, Young Pioneers, Komsomols—a host of organizations extended propaganda from the adult domain to the youth cohorts of society. The idealist educational philosopher Giovanni Gentile became Mussolini's minister of education and sought to implement his own educational ideals through the system of Fascist schools. In the United States schools assumed a special function: the integrating of foreigners into the immigrant nation. There was the ideal of a melting pot and the ideal of emergent Americanism. These ideals persist. Small American schoolchildren with hands upon their hearts still daily pledge allegiance to the flag. There is also a lively pre-emptive movement in the U.S.A. to establish English as the official language of that country by constitutional amendment. In short, anywhere and everywhere, there is a nationalist statist role for education. Education is expected to serve what might be called political moral imperatives.

The interbellum period also included the great economic depression of the 1930s, a worldwide slump wihch affected all nations and which only effectively ended with the outbreak of a second world war. Social experience in this period reinforced obvious linkages between the educational and the economic structures of society. The linkages were complex and embraced such contradictory factors as a newly created unemployed intelligentsia that constituted a political liability and established the notion that the education system, of whatever country, provides an avenue for upward social mobility, access to careers, and general opportunities for meritocratic betterment. Schools and colleges entrenched themselves as de jure guardians of entry to the professions and de facto guardians of access to the more rewarding work roles in society. This development was enhanced by the general increase in all sectors, public and private, of bureaucratization. The education system, public and private, consequently assumed a social function of gatekeeper and distributor of life chances amongst the oncoming generations. To the classical liberating purpose of education had now been added the modern function of sociological sorting.

After World War II there was a realignment of political power and a re-establishment of order. The interrelated and interdependent nature of the global economy and ecology became increasingly apparent and in the decades after 1945 technological advances in communication brought about a quasi-educational result described by McLuhan as the emergence of a "global village." Mass information is correlated with mass education and the obvious dependence of the new technology on educational bases, combined with the increased participation of adults in formal and informal educational experiences of all sorts, led to easy acceptance of the concept of lifelong learning. This at least was the perception in the developed nations; politicians clearly perceived the relationship between educational achievement and national status.

Paradoxically, this impetus toward state expenditures on education can, at least in part, be interpreted as a kind of reincarnation of the motivations of classical liberal education. To free men to pursue higher ends it was first necessary to liberate them from economic servitude. Looked at in this way, vocational training was itself a liberal art. Once economic ends were accomplished, the curriculum could then explode into all those areas now so typical of smorgasbord adult education: learning for personal and aesthetic or hedonic reasons rather than learning instrumental to job acquisition or credentialling.

Throughout these recent historical developments it has always been possible, in all countries, to observe a strong current of idealism amongst professional educators, even in the most pragmatic of societies. Thus Goodlad, in concluding his analysis of the purposes of American schools, declares an idealistic faith:

> Central to all that has preceded is my belief in the common school. I regard it not simply as desirable for but as essential to the preservation and cultivation of our democratic way of life and our political democracy. The fact that as individuals and as a nation we have not lived up to our ideals in no way diminishes either the attractiveness of these ideals or their continuing appeal in guiding our actions. Indeed, the obvious gap between the two should challenge the best in us all. The fact that our schools have too often reflected our shortcomings rather than our ideals is no justification for expecting little of them or doing away with them. It is, I think, no accident that this democracy still survives in spite of our errors of commission and omission, and that we have one of the most comprehensive, accessible systems of schooling in the world.[7]

This authority immediately goes on to say that *"The prime role of our schools is the development of the full potential of each individual"* (my italics).

And, from a contrasting standpoint, in Fascist Italy, the philosopher Gentile expounds:

> The school, this glorious inheritance of human experience, this ever-glowing hearth where the human spirit kindles and sublimates life as an object of constant criticism and of undying love, may be transformed, but cannot be destroyed.[8]

Such sentiments as these could be culled from the educational literature of every nation that possesses such a literature. Educational idealism knows no ideological boundaries. It seems fair to say, then, from the larger historical perspective, that education has about it an idealistic and humanistic quality which renders it distinctive and special among the occupations and callings of men. No other subset of human activity and organization possesses quite the same degree of commitment to the totality of purposes of mankind. Somehow education seems to be pre-requisite, co-requisite, and post-requisite to all of the other affairs, interests and occupations of culture. The crassest of politicians, the most banal of Babbits, will pay lip-tribute to this generality. Indeed one might well be forgiven for taking this argument to its limits and maintaining that education was the end that continued to be sought when all other subordinate ends such as security, health and wealth had been accomplished. As a learning species, the progeny of *homo educans* have gained the evolutionary advantage over all other species and massive dominion over the natural planetary environment. There is considerable consensus that the perpetuation of human species is now itself a very direct function of education and, hence, of educational leadership. The history of education also suggests that such leadership is likely to be imbued with a special degree of idealism, quite apart from any pragmatic concerns about survival.

The Constellation of Purposes

Education must ultimately be defined in terms of its ends, its purposes. These constitute its imperatives. They shape and dictate its means. Our survey of educational history, curtailed and abbreviated though it must be, illustrates the three strands of purpose which have governed the educational endeavor from earliest times. These strands can be classified as the aesthetic, the economic, and the ideological.

Aesthetic Education

By the aesthetic purposes of education are meant those ends primarily associated with self-fulfillment and the enjoyment of life. Much falls within this rubric. The basic curriculum remains that of the liberal arts and the humanities but it can also be said to include the tool subjects of literacy and numeracy as well as much of the content of adult education. Sports and the entertainment arts are likewise means to the aesthetic ends of education. The central classical idea of "liberation" remains a valid component of this strand of purpose even though modulated in a variety of hedonic and even utilitarian ways. We should neither discount, however, nor disvalue in any way the hedonic side of things; hedonism, the seeking of pleasure as distinct from the seeking of happiness, is a fundamental part of human nature. It cannot be dismissed as trivial. In practical terms this might mean that bridge classes for senior citizens are as honorable as the study of history by statesmen and scholars for the avoidance of future folly. Aesthetic purpose is however only rarely pure and more generally is inextricably intertwined with the other major strands of educational purpose.

Economic Education

All vocational education or training is economic in motivation. In crudest terms people undertake this sort of education with the manifest end of making money. The apex of this educational system is of course the universities where induction into the major professions is tightly controlled. The curriculum associated with this purposive strand permeates the entire spectrum of educational activity. Thus, while the first days of schooling may be construed as aesthetic wherein the aim is to impart initial literacy and numeracy to the learner, still this aim is also instrumental and prerequisite to further progress throughout the structured educational system and thus to the ultimate economic status of the learner. So in that advance educational nation, Japan, fierce competition begins as early as entry into kindergarten. It may indeed be liberating and rewarding for the Japanese infant to master his first thousand characters; it will certainly enhance his enjoyment of life, but it may also partially determine the capitalized yen value of his discounted lifetime earnings.

The interdependence between aesthetic and economic education can also be illustrated in the relations between, say, medical research and quality of life. Medical science is in general a highly remunerative and intensely professional occupation. The fruits of its labors, however, also redound to the extension of human life and improved capacity for the enjoyment of that life. In this sense it performs a liberating and aesthetic function; its purposive emphasis can be considered as aesthetic education at one remove. The same holds true for engineering, accounting, aviation and possibly all of the practical arts. Conceptually, however, there is a difference between learning to earn and earning to learn.

Ideological Education

It has always been a function of education to transmit the culture of the society in which it occurs. This has always been so. It is as true of aboriginal education as it is of the most advanced nation-state. The impulse to perpetuate and advance a nationalistic spirit, to inculcate rising generations with a nationalistic (or euphemistically *patriotic*) ethos is universal. It has been only mildly tempered, if at all, by the realities of international organizations such as the United Nations, or by the realities of multi-national conglomerates and cartels, or even by the stark realities of super-power nuclear weaponry. The thrust of this purposive aspect of education extends into all levels of educational structure although perhaps with a major emphasis in the earlier years of the educational process. As has been said apocryphally of Catholic educators, the principle seems to be, "Give me the first years of a child's life and I give you the man."

Although this purpose can be interpreted psychologically as in-group indoctrination it is usually complemented or supplemented by religious concerns which may themselves be either sacred or secular. Catholic nations seek to ensure the propagation of orthodoxy. Communist states consciously place education at the service of their political ideology. Fundamentalist Islam relies especially on Koranic schools. The rabbi is an archetypical educator in Judaic culture. Even the most liberal and laissez-faire of democratic countries look to their educational structures to imbue youth with at least a modicum of patriotic and citizenship ideals. Moreover, quite apart from any ideologies, there is a universal concern with moral education. Formal educational organizations share with the family a primary responsibility in this large and difficult task. It is well established that schools operate according to a hidden as well as an overt curriculum and these curricula reinforce each other in the perpetuation of an ethos or system of cultural values. All such education can be classified as serving the ideological strand of purpose. This aspect of purpose, given its direction toward the inner life and emotional experience of learners, given also the amenability of those learners to indoctrination, again supports the claim that education is a special sort of activity, closely akin to though not identical with the work of churches, synagogues, mosques and temples. Even in the most thoroughly secularized societies and in formally atheistic systems such as the Soviet Union, the moral dimension of ideological purpose persists. This fact carries over to the perceived status of administrators and leaders. It does not necessarily invest them with moral stature but it imposes upon them a subtle kind of onus that has a distinctive moral charge.

This third strand of purpose also rarely appears in pure form. Normally the aesthetic or economic emphases are salient. Even where the ideological purpose is clear-cut and dominant it is usually intertwined with and modulated by the other strands. It is this normal condition of confusion or mixing of purpose which goes to explain the general difficulty of polemic in the field of education. Administrators need to know the purposive source of criticisms that arise from various client and member groups. This may by no means be immediately apparent even to those who are themselves the source of complaint. Demands for foreign language training, for example, may be presented on cultural grounds or ideological grounds—a liberal belief in bilingualism for example (French in Canada, Spanish in the U.S.A.)—while the real motivations are economic (career opportunities for offspring). Furthermore, it becomes only too easy for the skilled rhetorician to shift the ground of argument from one strand of purpose to another in order to contest or confound the opposition.

The Special Nature of Education

Schools, colleges and universities have obvious differences from hospitals, factories, shops and barracks. The really crucial distinctions, however, run deep and are more profound. All human organizations, whether they are simple or complex, exist to achieve purposes. These purposes in turn are rooted in human desires or values. Each organization seeks to serve its members and its clientele by altering the world in such a way as to realize those values.

Military and police forces have a legal monopoly of violence granted them by the state so that they can achieve the desired state of security (by defending against enemies or controlling offenders). Here one can say the basic value is security. The medical establishment exists to maintain and promote public health; its basic value is health. Government with its ministries and bureaus exists to maintain and advance the general public welfare. Its basic value is the public interest. Commerce, trade and industry generate organizations whose fundamental purpose, whatever the rhetoric to the contrary, is to make a profit. The basic value here is wealth, economic wealth. Institutionalized religions seek through their organizational forms to promote and propagate their doctrines and actualize such values as salvation, liberation or enlightenment.

What then is the basic value of educational organization?

It can be seen from the foregoing that non-educational organizations subscribe primarily to one or the other of the three strands of educational purpose, whereas education subscribes to all of them. It seeks to establish and enhance the values of security, health, the common good, the interest of the state, the capacity for profit, wealth of all sorts and the highest values of philosophy, ideology and religion. It is in this sense the most general human pursuit. If we were to seek a term for the basic educational value we might call it fulfillment. This term is both sufficiently precise and sufficiently imprecise for the scope of our present analysis. Education has been shown to be a general set of human behaviors and experiences organized about three categories of purpose: aesthetic, economic, and ideological. It can also be said to subserve all human values and to be prerequisite to their fulfillment. It is this all-inclusive quality which makes education so special and, at the same time, so *human*. Because of this relevance to all aspects of the human condition, education is also invested from the outset with a moral character. Through it we are all inducted into the ethos of our particular culture. Through it we acquire our moral dimension. On it we depend for our livelihood and the quality of our life. And if education is this special then it follows that educational leadership ought likewise to be special. It is, in fact, a moral art.

This chapter argues that educational leaders should be aware of the deep roots of purpose which underlie their organizations. Analytically, these embrace three major strands of purpose: aesthetic, economic and ideological—purposes which in turn correlate with three types of value to be explicated later. Leadership is always a function of value and of commitment to organizational value or purpose.

In this chapter we have explored the question, What is education? In the next chapter we shall turn more directly to the question, What is educational leadership?

The Organization of Education

In the last chapter we explored the reasons for having formal education at all. These reasons are always philosophical, having to do with ends or terminal values as opposed to means or instrumental values. The means aspect of education presents a curious contrast to the ends aspect. Whereas the latter tends to be always conceptually cloudy, mixed in composition, and open to variable interpretation, the former is often simplistic in the extreme, especially when it comes to structure or organization. Strangely, too, the ultimate instrumentality of education, that which is referred to in the jargon as the teaching-learning process, is itself inordinately complex, subtle and ill-understood. The following quotation from the standpoint of educational psychology is indicative:

> ...Consider the hundreds of theoretical formulations, rational equations, mathematical models of the learning process that have accrued; the thousands of research studies. And *now* consider that there is still no wide agreement on the empirical conditions under which learning takes place, or even on the definition of learning and its relations to other psychological processes or phenomena. Consider also that after all this scientistic effort our actual *insight* into the learning process—reflected in every humanly important context to which learning is relevant—has not improved one jot.[1]

Yet while both ends (education) and means (teaching) are often unclear, they are linked in practice in very simple-minded ways. While much mystery still surrounds the teacher-learner/teaching-learning situation which is, as it were, the coal-face or cutting edge of educational productivity, it is rarely thought that the processes of funding, administration, and management of this situation ought to be in any way equally difficult, obscure or problematic. In fact, the pattern of organizational logic has changed little over the recorded time of educational history. Classes, classrooms, and the basic pedagogical arrangements—give or take the occasional technological embellishment or theoretical vogue—have remained fundamentally unaltered since classical times. Teachers talk, question, expound; students listen, answer, and succumb to distraction; exercises are performed and monitored, tests and examinations are set and graded; and the cycle repeats itself annually throughout the various levels of structure. The curriculum is organized into subject matter, the latter into courses, units, and lessons. The words of Ecclesiastes seem all too appropriate: "The thing that hath been, it is that which shall be; and that which is done is that which shall be done: and there is no new thing under the sun."

Education is conservative. That it is so very conservative is a point for leaders to bear continually in mind, for this essentially traditional character generates the phenomena of periodic waves of radical reaction. In the extreme case, proposals are even made for the total demolition of the established system; yet all these waves subside leaving in their wake the old edifice, modified perhaps, but in fact more conservatively entrenched than before. The common sense maxim to be derived is that leadership must always be judiciously cautious about overt commitments to radical enthusiasms. The record shows that they have a tendency to pass.

Between Shakespeare's schoolboy with his "satchel and shining morning face, creeping like snail unwillingly to school" and today's youth clambering aboard their yellow school buses, there is an uninterrupted affinity and continuity. Students continue to be dragooned into buildings and to respond with boredom and restiveness. Yet restive reaction, now as then, rarely amounts to rebellion. The counter-cultural excesses of the 1960s led to sit-ins in the offices of university presidents, student strikes, faculty disruptions, explosive rhetoric and rancor in the media, and even to tragic and fatal incidents of violence, but the end result has to be assessed, like it or not, as a form of public endorsement and affirmation of education as it is typically organized. Things do change, but they also remain the same. Education and all its organizational manifestations would seem to be one of the grand permanences of the human condition.

The consistency of public attitudes over time can be easily illustrated. The following quotations respectively, from Aristotle in the 30s of the fourth century B.C. and Adolf Hitler in the 30s of the twentieth century A.D. show this:

At present opinion is divided as to the proper tasks of education. Not everyone is agreed about what should be learned by the young.... If we look at actual practice, confusing questions arise; and it is not at all clear whether the proper studies to be followed are those which are morally edifying or those which advance the bounds of knowledge. Each sort of study receives some votes in its favor.[2]

...the youthful brain should in general not be burdened with things 95% of which it cannot use and hence forgets again.... in many cases, the material to be learned in the various subjects is so swollen that only a fraction of it remains in the head of the individual pupil, and only a fraction of this abundance can find application, while on the other hand it is not adequate for the man working and earning his living in a definite field.[3]

This stability of debate about education over time is reflected in a corresponding stability of educational organization. The ways in which educational means are organized to accomplish educational ends are consistently stable and far from infinite in variety. It is these structural arrangements, rather than methodology and attitudes, which are our present concern.

Educational Structure

Formal education is typically accomplished through familiar modes of organization such as schools, colleges, institutes and universities. These in turn are ordered by the organizing categories of funding, chronology, purpose and governance.

Funding for an organization may be public, private or mixed. Quantitatively the public category is the most important. Education today is a major function of any developed state and a major competitor, together with national defense, health and social services for budgetary allocations of resources. Legally there is a general recognition of the citizens' right to education at public cost for a given number of years. How many years and at what level of burden on the treasury are questions with variable answers: from the guarantee of Ph.D. level in Kuwait to a more general norm in North America of about ten years of public schooling. Suggestions have been made, for example, that the school leaving age in California should be raised to twenty-one but, more typically, that statutory age is set between fourteen and sixteen years of age. In any event, publicly funded education in some measure has become universally regarded as a right rather than a privilege and, furthermore, (though somewhat paradoxical in logic) a compulsory right. Education is both free and compulsory. It is also often simultaneously conducted through private means (where it becomes non-compulsory and non-free).

The much smaller number of private as opposed to public organizations cannot be discounted, for they are frequently of great prestige or specially renowned for educational accomplishment or innovation. Institutions such as Stanford, Harvard, Oxbridge, Eton, Harrow, Summerhill, Juilliard can each be rightly considered as having some claim to educational leadership. Frequently, too, it is cogently argued that this leadership is itself a function of freedom from the controls and constraints that come with government or public financing. Often, however, these private institutions are in direct or indirect receipt of public funds and their classification might more properly be described as mixed. The mixed category is especially large where, for example, the state subsidizes, directly or indirectly, religious or parochial schooling.

Finally there are those organizations which depend entirely upon the marketplace and private sources for their financial support. Trade schools, daycare centers, Montessori schools are examples. Nevertheless, these too cannot expect to escape entirely from the monitoring power of the state and, one way or another, the public, through the organs of government, exercise a continuous aegis over all the forms of educational structure.

Education is also structured chronologically in the familiar groupings of primary, secondary and tertiary. Primary education covers the years from pre-school and kindergarten through to statutory entrance to the secondary level, normally at the end of grades six or seven, i.e., approximately ages eleven to thirteen in the North American pattern. The secondary years continue through to the statutory school leaving age and to entrance into tertiary or higher education. While the first two chronological periods are fairly well defined, the tertiary is much less so. Its clientele may be drawn from throughout the remainder of the life-span although, because of considerable emphasis upon the economic purposes of education, there is some tendency to a clustering at the earlier end of the age spectrum. This phase includes not only colleges, technical and vocational institutes and universities but also the whole polymorphous range of adult education from night schools and Volkschule to the in-service and on-site training provided by private industry and the military.

The governance aspect of structure refers simply to the level of authority (federal government, state, county, school district, region) which assumes responsibility for provisions of the educational service. It may range from the single entrepreneurial ownership of a private school through to national and even international jurisdictions (e.g., United World Colleges). Although this might seem to be an unambiguous source of structure it can, in reality, at times be misleading. Thus, in Canada for example, while the federal government is specifically declared to have no constitutional authority in the field of education (British North America Act, 1867) in fact that level of government operates and maintains schools such as those funded by the Departments of National Defence and Indian Affairs and, through indirect financing, intrudes into the operation of universities and vocational schools. Likewise, in the United States, the practice of federal cost sharing (Elementary and Secondary Education Act, 1965) provides a means by which leadership at one level of governance can be confused with that being exercised at another.

Finally, the purposive principles of education dealt with in general terms in the preceding chapter translate into generalized (and occasionally specific) mission statements for the organizations set up to accomplish the declared purposes. However, it can be noted that the conservative character of education again results in little variety of structure. Obviously medical training may require elaborate facilities such as teaching hospitals with expensive and complex technological services, and a school of aviation may need access to an airfield and aircraft, but even in these cases the basic logic of pedagogical structure persists with classrooms, labs and teachers. Even the apparent innovations provided by correspondence schools and television universities such as Great Britain's Open University, or such unorthodox graduate arrangements as the American Nova and Walden doctorate programs are, upon analysis, merely variations and reaffirmations of orthodox and traditional practices.

What has to be appreciated as historically new is that when all the varieties of educational organization are taken together, the human involvement in educational activity is massive and costly. It is occasionally referred to as the largest national industry of modern times; in the 1970s it was estimated for the United States that between a quarter and a half of the population was engaged in education.[4] Certainly, for every modern nation education is both a very big business and a central function of the state. Its pervasive nature and its influence upon all citizens throughout their lives endows it with profound value, moral and ethical significance. Some of the value problems deriving from structure alone will be considered below.

Problems

There is no need to describe the general forms of organizational structure in education since they are already familiar to every reader. Variations in specific forms are either known directly in situ or are accessible from published material. What is of more interest from the valuational standpoint is the sheer size and scope of the overall educational project, however it is translated into administrative-managerial structures.

This is most clearly visible in public education. The business of public education is now so large and universal that it must be classified as an institution, along with the other entrenched institutions of family, military, police, and state bureaucracy. It follows that serving members of this institution will tend to become imbued, consciously or unconsciously, with the stable institutional values of the educational project. Characteristically these values are conservative, defensive of the status quo, and inertial or resistant to change. Another value feature of the educational institution is familiarity. Because of its pervasiveness the workings, mores and values of education are well known. This is notoriously so in that all citizens of a modern state have been to school, most of them to public school, and while the adage that familiarity breeds contempt need not necessarily be taken too literally the fact remains that education holds little mystery from the standpoint of its organizational structures, administration and methods.

Despite the occasional radical proposal[5] to deschool society and dismantle formal educational structures it remains true that, by and large, at least a decade of the most formative years of a citizen's life is spent attending schools and this may be taken as a minimal estimate. The saw, "twenty years learning and forty years earning" reveals a conventional wisdom already somewhat outdated. In the 1960s, for example, it was seriously mooted that the Californian school-leaving age be raised to twenty-one.

This pervasive impress of the educational institution combined with its heavy charge on the public treasury is enough, even without any ideology about the necessity and benefits of education (now almost univerally accepted as an unexamined value assumption), to create a powerful political lobby and a massive vested interest. This entails that anyone aspiring to lead in this field must acquire some considerable political sophistication.

Public education is organized as a complex of organizational systems arranged in well-defined patterns. The basic unit is the school, itself subdivided into classes. Schools are aggregated into school districts; districts in turn into state or national systems. At each level from school on upwards, "ownership" input may be made into the administrative governance subsystem, typically through boards of trustees or governors, committees of local government and, ocasionally, direct central or regional government bureaucracy. Ultimately, power and authority are legally assigned to the electorate. Politically, this is exercised through representatives at each level culminating in the eminent domain of the state itself. The combination of size, scope, cost and importance of the overall system ensures a powerful bureaucracy which in turn, from characteristics of bureaucracy to be considered in the next chapter, ensures a quality of inertial conservatism and resistance to change.

It should be noted that while these factors apply quite differently, if at all, to private education there too, for quite different reasons (such as elitism and perpetuation of tradition), a value orientation is found that is resistant to radical change and amenable to a conversative spirit. Even schools with overtly permissivist and radical philosophies will tend to resist any change to *those* philosophies and their attendant administrative styles.

Each important human constituency within the institution: students, administrators, faculty, taxpayers, must be considered as a stakeholder or value-interest group which seeks to exert and extend its hold on the common good. That good is ostensibly (and rhetorically) education but, as we have seen, the concept is often unspecified, confused or empty. In practical terms it amounts to a fiscal flow of costs (operating, capital, and salaries) and a qualitative-quantitative flow of benefits (knowledge, culture, employment). Because each component group has a natural tendency to see or portray itself as the stakeholder of prime importance, it is not logically or politically surprising that the *common* interest, the goal of *education*, is selectively reinterpreted by each special interest with corresponding distortions in the institutional reward system and in the overall system flow of costs and benefits. Such distortions, which are a function of the political power of respective stakeholders in any given context, lead to what Hardin[6] and others have referred to as the problem of the commons. We shall return to discussion of this difficulty below. For now we can note that each institutional subsystem has its own built-in intrinsic value problem, namely, competition for scarce institutional resources which have alternative uses and claimants.

The chronological ordering of educational structure—primary, secondary, tertiary—also implies a built-in means-ends relationship between the parts of the structure and hence, since each successive end becomes the means for a subsequent end, there is a corresponding status structure. A higher status value attaches to university and college than to elementary or junior-secondary sybsystems. This, too, can lead to subtle and not-so-subtle forms of value conflict within the institution. Blame for the failure of college students to possess adequate language skills is often back-tracked down the system to the elementary and primary levels. Conversely, stress on college entrance can be derogated by school administrators as elitist or dysfunctional with respect to vocational training and youth employment. Inter-subsystem rivalries coexist with intra-subsystem conflicts as, for example, in the tension within universities between the teaching and research functions. In 1986 the U.S. commissioner of education criticized the prestigious Harvard University for doing a bad job of teaching, while in 1983 the American Association for the Advancement of Science reported panic in scientific circles over the ability of the school system to maintain America's status as a technological great power.

When educational structure is considered from the standpoint of purpose (aesthetic, economic, or ideological), the critical value problem centers on justification. Educational purposes are always politically open. They are also subject to what economists call opportunity cost, that is, the price of achieving one objective may be the loss of achieving other desirable objectives. This means that purposes are more philosophical and strategic as contrasted with the goals that they generate, which are more managerial and tactical. This open-endedness of purposes and the necessity for intention, commitment and will to translate them into goals means that purposes are endlessly subject to debate, critique and argument throughout the polity. This debate about ends rather than means is the true educational debate and is responsive to changes in cultural, political and socio-economic conditions. When graduates of the public system cannot find employment or when sexual problems (AIDS, teen-age pregnancy) assume socio-political proportions, the debate about the purposes of education becomes enlivened. If sufficiently intense it can result in changes in the structure to reflect the corresponding changes in educational philosophy. Any purposive emphasis can be challenged: the academic for irrelevance, the vocational for redundancy, the ideological for heresy or economic incompetence—and the critique can have structural implications as purposes are translated into goal achievement systems. The educational leader has therefore to be not merely aware of the state of debate, the debate itself being endless, but also an active participant within it. The leader cannot be a cipher or a mere factotum, as is the image of the value-neutered public servant but must stand for something and, if need be, fall by what that value stands for. The leader has also to be ready at any time to voice and express the purposive emphases to which he and his organization subscribe. And this in turn means that the leader should have thought through his value positions. There are two bounden duties: to know where the organization stands (a matter of rational analysis) and to be committed to that stand (a matter of personal values).

Finally, when considering structure from the standpoint of governance and funding, we are returned to the problem of the commons mentioned earlier. Different levels of governance make up a hierarchy of ascending collective concerns. Where conflict arises between levels the moral logic is deceptively simple; the lower (school, school district) yields to the higher (county, region, province or state) up to the ultimate level of the nation state wherein resides the final authority and taxing power. In short, lesser interests should yield to greater. This arrangement places the state at the apex of the moral hierarchy, in a position of supervising the commonwealth. The ethical problem created by this is that each interested individual or interest group or level will tend in practice to seek to maximize its share of the commons or of the overall reward system.

Hardin's[7] statement of this problem draws the analogy with common grazing pasture wherein each herder rationally seeks to maximize his grazing even though that will result in the destruction of the commons and a total loss in the end for each individual. Similarly, in underdeveloped countries there is no incentive to control the birth rate since it is prudential for each set of parents to maximize offspring even though this can destroy the commons for all. Unless Draconian measures are instituted and enforced by the state, as in the People's Republic of China, the commonwealth cannot be saved.

Returning to public education, the same problem arises with respect to demands on the public purse. Each level and group will militate for maximum rather than optimum allocation of resources for its own interest, and in a field such as education, where purposes and goals are unclear, the potential for opportunism is obvious. This natural tendency is reinforced, as we shall see, by the compartmentalizing mode of advocacy behavior in modern bureaucracy. As Pastin pessimistically remarked, "As long as we view ourselves as rationally self-interested individuals playing against the reward system" there is no hope of ethically responsible conduct.[8]

The intimate connection between power, political power (itself a value), and the resolution of commons problems emphasizes the necessity for the educational leader to have political skills and to be, in part at least, a politician. This in itself, of course, entails no guarantee of ethical responsibility; it only recognizes that without understanding of and access to the hierarchy of political decision making, ethical responsibility may simply be impossible.

Loss of ethics is also a general feature of all complex organizations or bureaucracies simply because collective decision making, power and authority lead to diffusion of responsibility. This is a point we shall deal with at length in parts II and III of this book but for now it can be noted that the legal principle that "One cannot hang a Common Seal" means that (as anyone who has long served on committees well knows) it is difficult or impossible to pinpoint responsibility for any organizational decision on a single "hangable" individual. Diffusion of power and dissipation of responsibility tend to psychologically abstract and depersonalize all organizational structures. This is especially true of the large bureaucratic systems of modern public education.

Finally, there is the central moral problem of self-interest. We have seen how with the "problem of the commons" this can be damaging to the community, to the collectivity and to organizations, but self-interest also operates within as well as without organizations. Each of us can be assumed to act out of perceptions of our own self-interest at all times, but for this assumption to hold we need to take a sophisticated view of the *self* incorporated in the concept of self-interest.

The first thing to note is that the self is thoroughly amorphous. Analytically one cannot isolate and locate it with any degree of precision. The second thing to note is that it has extensions. Multiple extensions. Rarely if ever do we encounter pure selfishness or pure ego. Instead the ego is extended through psychological identification with kin, friends, relatives and an infinity of other associations; even to such grossly inflated proportions as when IRA or Hezbolla fanatics identify themselves with Ireland or Islam respectively. At more ordinary levels of identification we find that the norm within organizations is for conflict between extended egos. Outside formal organizations mothers identify (to the point of self-sacrifice of life) with their offspring; lovers identify with lovers; families with clans, tribes and nations. Identification of the self is thus polymorphous and perverse. This means that any realistic interpretation of the value structure of organizations must allow for this complexity, a complexity where overlapping and conflicting fields of interest are superimposed upon the basic cooperative structure of formal roles. Figure 1 depicts the classical formal structure of organization which of course, at any of the stages, may be supplemented by staff input to complete the line-and-staff logic implicit and virtually universal in all basic organizational forms. Figures 2 and 3 apply this logic to the school situation. Simplifying greatly and considering for the purposes of illustration only students, teachers, and administrators the "circles of interest" show how these extend differentially for each group. Administrators are buffered from students by teachers; teachers consider students their primary concern as opposed to administrators; and administrators find the teaching staff interposed between them and the student clientele. Figure 2 is again oversimplified because, while it represents the circles of interest of three educational organizational roles with respect to each, it makes no representation of the other multiple interests of role incumbents (e.g., with peers, parents, family, etc.) and makes no representation of the interaction between these roles, an interaction which cannot be captured merely

FIGURE 1

Formal Role Structure and Hierarchy

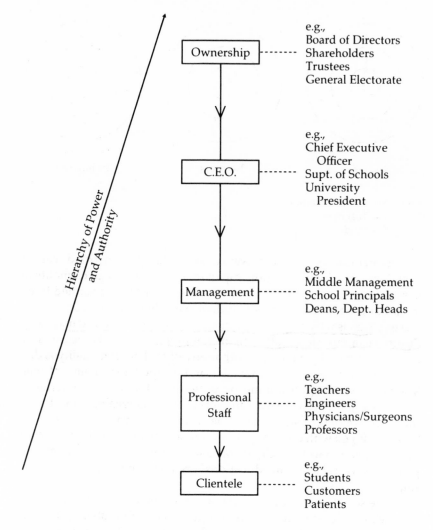

by the logic of a Venn diagram such as that shown in figure 3. Indeed, to represent the richness of value overlay and interplay and the potentialities for conflict of interest and organizational dysfunction as well as for intensification of interest and organizational synergy it would require a model extending into n-dimensional space and any gain of accuracy or predictability would be long lost through the sheer hypercomplexity of the representations.

FIGURE 2

Circles of Interest

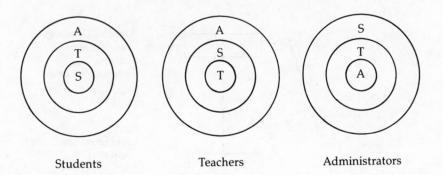

Students   Teachers   Administrators

Key: A —Administrators
      T —Teachers
      S —Students

Organization charts, however painstakingly construed, can at best depict the formal relationship of roles from which all elements of personality and value have been abstracted. Parts are assumed to be interchangeable. A student is a student, a teacher a teacher, a trustee a trustee. That is why organization charts tell us very little and may even disinform or misinform rather than enlighten. Each role is occupied by a flesh-and-blood personality with motivation. This personality is distinguished by values and character and an ineffable quality of will. Moreover, each is quite unique in a profoundly human way and therefore impossible to replace with any sort of interchangeable clone. Every time a personnel change is made the entire chemistry of the organization is changed with the changes ramifying outward from that place on the organizational chart. Organizational chemistry is value chemistry and it is a critical factor in educational organizations and their leadership.

The social reality of organizations, of life in organizations, cannot then be mapped or abstracted in the rigorous way desirable if scientific or even quasi-scientific claims are to be established. Self-interest, as we have seen, is not a straightforward or simple matter. Perhaps the only assertion that can be made of it with any certainty is that it will at some time enter into conflict with other self-interests within the organization. In other words, value conflict can be safely assumed to be a built-in feature of all organizational life. The management and modulation of this conflict as well as the political art of capitalizing upon it fall to the lot of the leader. Ethics becomes inescapable.

FIGURE 3

Intersecting Circles of Interest

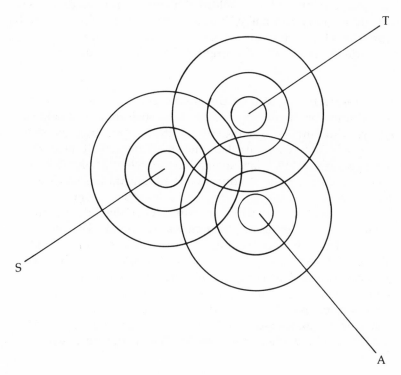

Key: A—Administrators
      T—Teachers
      S—Students

Within the discipline of educational administration a debate has extended over the last decade in which this fact about the phenomenological reality of educational life has only properly been grasped by Greenfield and his supporters.[9] Greenfield's opponents, notably Griffiths, Hills, and Willower, while modifying their opposition and seeking an accommodation with the new perspective, have been reluctant to abandon the possibility of an organizational science or at least the ultimate discovery of such lawlike generalities about human nature and behavior as will permit some measure of predictability in organization theory. Such views are consonant with scientific orthodoxy: "At present, the orthodox approach to biology is given by the mechanistic theory of life: living organisms are regarded as physico-chemical machines, and all the phenomena of life are considered to be explicable in principle in terms of physics and chemistry."[10]

Greenfield's emphasis on the salience of the feelings, actions, beliefs, purposes and values of role incumbents was criticized at first as being rudimentary and naive,"[11] but his view eventually came to be accepted as at least one of the necessary ways of looking at educational organization.[12] The state of current debate can be summarized as follows:

> Some researchers search for the great theory of educational administration or the paradigm that will transform it as a field of study, while others are content to offer elegant fragments of theory which may help explain one small piece at a time of the practitioner's reality. Some demand a more scientifically rigorous approach to the field of educational administration (Willower sees the field maturing in this regard), while others are not certain that this direction may be most fruitful (Greenfield doubts that science can ever guide the administrator's hand). The tension persists. The debate is prolonged. What is not in dispute is the picture of the educational administrator's world that is provided by recent studies—a workplace of constant movement, activity, simultaneous events, and tremendously diverse individuals and groups of people. It is a world of pressing practical problems which need to be solved, a world in which the attempt at problem solving will be made either with or without the aid of explicit theory.[13]

Theory and Practice

The dichotomy revealed above is more properly a *tri*chotomy. Not two things: theory and practice, but three things: theory, practice and *praxis*. Administration is not art or science; nor is it art and science, it is art, science, and *philosophy*.

All of this goes back to Aristotle, who taught what our present-day schools of administrative and organization theory seem to have forgotten, namely, that there are three ways of knowing and dealing with the world, three modes of action. He called them *theoria, techné and praxis*. The most abstract and pure of these is *theoria*, theory. It abstracts and generalizes by induction, deduction and hypothesis from the unruly world of sense data. Theory applied becomes *techné* or technics, techniques and technology. It can be noted that the practical world of techniques always stems from and feeds back to theory; there is no true dichotomy between theory and practice, each is but a different modality of a single continuum.

Finally there is *praxis*. Aristotle intended the term to mean ethical action in a political context, or purposeful human conduct, or behavior informed and guided by purposes, intentions, motives, morals, emotions and values *as well as* the facts or "science" of the case. Praxis is a deceptively obvious concept. It clearly applies to all administration, but it implies a duality in action, two "moments": one of consciousness or reflection in the first moment and one of action and commitment in the second moment. The modern distinction between behavior and action is itself too crude to capture the sense of praxis. Behavior is discernible movement, measurable movement, while action is movement with intent. Praxis therefore suggests the conscious reflective intentional action of man, as opposed to mere reflex or mechanical responses to stimuli. The educational leader whose time is all spent dealing with emergent problems, like a firefighter running from fire to fire, is not likely to be engaged in praxis. The best that could be accomplished would be a sort of pragmatic application of techné: this practice worked before, let's try it again. Such an administrator is not leading and, more accurately, is following or being led. The concept of praxis is important, therefore, to round out our understanding of organizational action. It is, in fact, the central subject matter of this book.

The Field of Action

Lord Snow, famous for his description of two cultures alien to each other, the culture of science and the culture of letters, has also drawn an important distinction between the man of science and the man of action.[14] The mode of science is to pursue a single topic with great intensity for long periods of time with painstaking deliberation, observation, and reflection. In contrast, the mode of action, that is, the mode of management, is to treat many things with superficial attention for very short periods of time with highly constrained opportunities, if any, for deliberation, detached observation and reflection. The contrast here is between theoria and praxis—not between theory and practice but between theory and *praxis*. The implication is plain enough. As Getzels puts it, "... the basic *operational* model in the present analysis of administrative processes in the educational context is composed of these three salient factors: the interaction of *role* and *personality* in the context of *value*."[15] The educational leader is caught up in a field of values in which he is forced to choose and act. the extent and nature of this field can be shown in a diagram (Figure 4). Overlapping and subsuming levels of value (V_1–V_5) extend upwards and downwards from the individual (V_1) through his immediate organizational associations in the informal organizations (e.g., teachers who form a friendly peer group on the staff V_2) to the organization itself with its overt and covert

FIGURE 4

The Field of Action

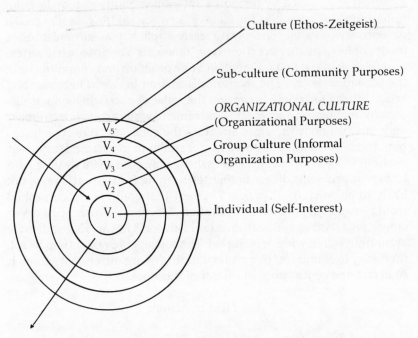

Culture (Ethos-Zeitgeist)

Sub-culture (Community Purposes)

ORGANIZATIONAL CULTURE
(Organizational Purposes)

Group Culture (Informal
Organization Purposes)

Individual (Self-Interest)

purposes (e.g., the school V_3) to the subculture of the community in which the school is embedded (V_4) and finally the given social culture in space and time which is a function of geography and history and is experssed in those values represented by the German concept of the spirit of the times (*Zeitgeist* V_5).

Within this field of value action the educational leader must seek to establish a praxis. The complexity is a given. The difficulty is a given. The oftentimes anguish and the alltimes potential for stress upon the actors are givens. No one maintains that leadership is easy. If it should seem to be so, then beware. In all probability something is, or is about to be, going wrong.

Conclusion

All organizations and institutions are value-ridden, but the peculiar moral-ethical quality of the educational institution derives from the concept of education itself and from its appropriation by the state. The intrusion by the educational state into the early lives of citizens and the perpetuation of this presence throughout the remainder of the life cycle, especially when it is organized about the economic and ideological sets of educational purposes, means in practice that educational administrators are continually making decisions which are directly or indirectly crucial to the fulfillment of individual human projects. That is to say, the human condition and the quality of life are inextricably dependent on the educational institution and its component organizations. In blunt language, schools can make or break people. Moreover, the institution is the means by which social values are entrenched and perpetuated and the means by which culture is transmitted. All of which makes it an intensely moral enterprise and suggests that educational leadership can well be morally onerous. Moral and value difficulties arise through each of the purposive aspects of educational organization and through built-in conflicts of interest and value of dysfunctions stemming from bureaucratic modes of organization. Arguments about theory and about a perceived rift between theory and practice necessitate our reconsidering the Aristotelian concept of praxis. Educational praxis deals with the complex field of value interactions that permeates educational organization and praxis is at the core of the art of leadership.

We shall next examine more closely the nature of leadership itself. Chapters 3 to 7 will be devoted to this scrutiny and in chapters 8 to 11 we shall return more directly to the theme of values and morality, synthesizing at that time the theory and philosophy of educational leadership and praxis.

II
Leadership

3

The Nature of Leadership/
Administration

Administration is a casually used word and leadership is a much abused word. The latter has over one hundred serious definitions.[1] It has also been castigated as an "incantation for the bewitchment of the led."[2] Yet leadership is, as a concept, not so much vacuous as protean, impenetrable, elusive and delusive. All of which makes it very difficult to handle in any rigorous manner; yet, if our present task is to discuss the moral leadership of education, there is no escape from grappling with the conceptual difficulties involved. For that reason we shall devote this chapter to a general treatment of leadership/administration and the subsequent chapters 4 to 7 to more specific treatments of what can generally be called the leadership problem.

It is a prerequisite of intelligent discourse that an understanding be established as soon as possible between the parties to the discourse as to the essential meaning of their basic terms. Unless there is agreement about these, further discussion is vain. Much of the modern thrust of philosophy has been devoted to just this, the clarification of language in the attempt to resolve or relieve, *pace* Wittgenstein, the 'intellectual cramps' which give rise to pseudo-problems and philosophical perplexities.

The limits of my language are the limits of my world.[3]

What we cannot speak about we must pass over in silence.[4]

Conceptual confusion in the discussion about leadership is especially chronic and pathological. By and large administators and those who write about administration are not trained in the techniques of modern philosophical analysis nor, again by and large, can they be said to be particularly amenable to philosophical or abstract or "intellectual" interests. (Chester Barnard is a most significant exception to this latter generalization.) This is not to suggest that administrators are philistines, but to emphasize once again the different purview of their role. The philosophical *Weltanschauung* is a luxury which they might like to have but do not think that they can afford. And, correspondingly, it may well be argued that the professional philosophers of our day are unpractised, unskilled and ignorant in the arts of action.[5] Can these twain—men of action and men of contemplation—ever be reconciled?

In the Hindu epic poem, the *Bhagavadgita,* the protagonist is an archetypical administrator, the prince and general Arjuna who, of a sudden and upon the very field of battle or action, has an overwhelming failure of nerve. He begins to question his role and to wish that perhaps he should be a philosopher instead of a man of action, yet the divine instruction which he then receives is that the way of understanding and knowledge (in our terms, science and theory) and the way of action and duty (in our terms, management and administration) are indeed different, but they tend to the same end. Praxis, the theme of our study, requires that this end or union between ethics and action be considered *a priori,* in advance of action. In the realm of morals it is not enough to proceed backwards into the future, forever seeking to remedy the ill effects of our actions after the event. That is mere pragmatics. Ethics requires commitment *in advance.* Such an ethical commitment would also require a common language, a common understanding about the terms of discourse and, in the present case, an agreement about certain central concepts, namely: management, administration and leadership.

Administration and Management

The difference in usage between these terms, administration and management, is to some extent a matter of semantic convention. Usage differs, for example, on each side of the Atlantic, but for our purposes here the difference can be clarified by a figure. These selected aspects do not, of course, exhaust the manifold complexity of administration/ management, but they serve to illustrate the basic distinction, a systemic distinction, between the activities more properly ascribed to administration and those more properly ascribed to the lower systemic level of management. Certain points about this distinction are worth noting.

First, the usage as previously noted is a matter of linguistic convention. There is now, for example, a tendency in Great Britain to regard management as the higher function, despite anomalies such as the Royal Institute of Public Administration and the superior ranking of the administrative class to that of the managerial-professional class

FIGURE 1

Differentiating Aspects of Administration/Management

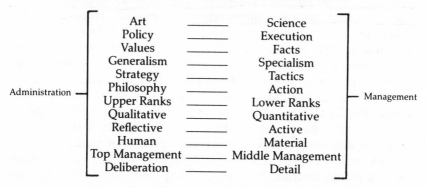

Administration		Management
Art	————	Science
Policy	————	Execution
Values	————	Facts
Generalism	————	Specialism
Strategy	————	Tactics
Philosophy	————	Action
Upper Ranks	————	Lower Ranks
Qualitative	————	Quantitative
Reflective	————	Active
Human	————	Material
Top Management	————	Middle Management
Deliberation	————	Detail

in the British Civil Service. Our usage is generally consistent with North American terminology.[6] In general, principals, headmasters, presidents and deans tend to regard themselves, without self-conscious analysis, as administrators rather than managers. It may also be noted that the great classical writings of Chester I. Barnard[7] tend to elide the semantic problem by talking of executives and executive functions, a usage which has now crystallized in the chief executive officer, often aspired to by school superintendents.

Second, it should be understood that the term administration subsumes management. Management is both subtended from and subsumed by the larger concept of administration. This is because the latter systemically embraces and generates the former, and because neither set of functions can exist in practice in discrete isolation from the other.

Third, because administration is hierarchically (systemically) superior and prior to management, this does not entail a value judgment that the former is somehow better than the latter. In fact, organizations can persist longer without administration than they can without management and on this criterion management would represent the better set of functions. Value judgments can, of course, be made if the criteria are specified.

Fourth, the terminological differentiation is a matter of emphasis and the joint administrative/management set of processes permeates the entire organization. The working day of any educator will be occupied with both kinds of activities at different times. Moreover all organization members of whatever rank will from time to time find themselves engaged in administrative acts, while all administrators will find much of their time occupied with strictly managerial tasks.

The usefulness of the distinction lies in its discriminatory power about organizational functions. The more one is involved with behaviors that bear on the ends, aims and purposes of the organization, the more one is engaged in administration. Likewise, the more general the value component in decision making and the more decisions affect the formulation and definition of organizational purpose, the more administrative and the less managerial such decision making becomes. In this light, it can be seen that classroom teaching tends to the managerial end of the spectrum, but it is also clear that teaching per se has many administrative features and can never be divorced entirely from administration/management. It is fair to say that a professional teacher is an administrator who is heavily involved in classroom management. In other words, teaching cannot rightly be reduced to a merely technical organizational function. This point is of special importance when we consider the ethical and moral responsibilities of teachers.

Administration can be defined as that general form of human behavior which seeks to achieve ends through organizational means. As these means are specified they give rise to technology and to the management of technology. Because of the commonality of problems encountered and strategies adopted in administration,[8] it can be described as a generalism in contrast to the increasingly specialist requirements of management. This is shown by the fact that at the highest systemic levels administrators pass easily from one complex organization to another, as when a general becomes a university president or a minister of finance takes up the portfolio of foreign affairs. On the other hand, a factory manager would not be expected to pass easily into the administration (as opposed to the management) of a school or college.

A final noteworthy point is this. Anyone, in principle, can do administration. Not anyone, either in principle or in practice, can do management. Administration demands no esoteric knowledge or training. On the contrary, it is the especial province of the amateur, as opposed to the professional expert. More, it is an entrenched and hallowed canon of Anglo-Saxon constitutional theory that the expert, the professional, should be "on tap and not on top." So the ultimate governance and authority for policy making in educational organizations is neither legally nor theoretically the professional staff of teachers and administrators but rather the boards of laypeople variously styled as trustees, governors, councils and the like.

Of course, in this sense, because anyone can administer it does not necessarily follow that anyone can administer well. (They may in fact administer badly but be saved by good management or, conversely, they may administer well but be subverted by bad management.) The arts of good administration have suggested to some the desirability of a preparatory background in the skills of generalism, which in turn has been interpreted at various times and in various places as implying a rigorous training in the humanities, for example: the classical Chinese mandarin system; the British civil service administrative caste drawn from candidates with a background in Oxbridge classicism; the French intellectual elitism typified in the *Ecole Normale d'Administration*. Still, even these schemes of preparation have been intended for those senior public servants who function at the apex of bureaucratic hierarchy and who are not themselves *carte blanche* administrators but powerful organizational executives who interface with the untrained and randomly skilled representatives of the *vox populi*.

In contrast, management skills are both specific to organizations, applicable only on site, yet general enough to admit of technical training and preparation, the moreso as social science delivers on some of its promises to explain and predict organizational behavior and as technology in general, greatly advanced by computerology, permits the determination and resolution of organizational problems of materiel, personnel, and accounting. As one approaches the managerial end of the administrative spectrum, it is reasonable to expect a correlation between efficiency and effectiveness, on the one hand, and background skills and preparation on the other. It is less possible to expect any such facile correlation in matters of administration.

Leadership

It is now possible for us to perceive that "leadership" is a vague term encompassing both administration and management as we now understand that process. Its vagueness opens it to all sorts of rhetorical manipulation and elsewhere I have discounted the term by proposing that leadership is a mere incantation for the bewitchment of the led.[9] It is a truism that no educational administrator would freely admit to not being a leader. On the contrary, the administrator would tend to conceive of the role of leader simply by way of definition. For our purposes, the term can then be used synonymously with administration. Administration *is* leadership. Leadership *is* administration.[10] The reader can check the validity of this assertion by substituting "administration" for "leadership" wherever and whenever the latter term is encountered in the literature. It will be seen that it is always possible to do this and, furthermore, with some gain in conceptual precision, as well as leaving the leadership incantation free for rhetorical use or even for mere elegant variation.

In the remainder of the text I shall use the term leadership with this understanding of its synonymy.

Bureaucracy

Modern state-financed education is essentially bureaucratic in its structure. The characteristic features of such structure are a hierarchy of personnel, tenure and careerism, role formalism, recordkeeping and paperwork, impartial and impersonal rules and regulations, professionalism and technical competence, committees and collective decision making, judicial process and unresponsiveness to changes in external or internal environment.[11] Educational administrators as leaders have to work within such a system and it follows they should understand it, especially its powerful impress of ethos, mores and norms, whereby the system itself can constrain and delimit all ethical action. The following excerpt from *Time Magazine* reveals an instance of the extent to which an administrator with an understanding of the bureaucratic machinery (here a U.S. government official) can influence the resolution of the highest ethical issues:

> Friends and critics call Assistant Secretary of Defense Richard Perle by many names—Prince of Darkness, Darth Vader, evil genius—and the witty Perle loves them all. By title, Richard (as he is invariably referred to in Washington) is merely one of eleven Assistant Secretaries, a *third-echelon* Pentagon *aide*. In practice, Perle is widely acknowledged to be a *major architect* of U.S. arms-control policy, though to his opponents he is a bureaucratic Machiavelli who *deviously torpedoed* all reasonable prospects for agreement. (My Italics.)[12]

It can also be noted as a classic illustration of the ethical importance of bureaucratic skills that Josef Stalin was able, from his position as general secretary of the Communist party of the Soviet Union to completely subvert and reinterpret the organization founded by Lenin. In general, the power of educational bureaucracies to determine their destinies in their own interest, despite attempts at external control, is a commonplace, but this does not relieve the administrator of the necessity to study the underlying dysfunctions.

The Power of Rationality

The guiding principle of bureaucracy, its metavalue (Chap. 9), is rationality. Its claim to superior efficiency and effectiveness rests on a prior claim to the superior deployment of reason in decision making, policy analysis, and organizational structure and function. It is also fair to say that a spirit of rationalism has always invested administration and co-operative endeavor if only because ends and means are connected by a causal logic. Once magic, superstition and theology are discounted as causal factors, one is left with those connections between cause and effect attributable to logic, mathematics and science. The modern emphasis upon logical rationality began with the concept of scientific management formulated by Frederick W. Taylor.[13] This logic, still unrefuted, is that there must be *one best way* of doing work. If a task can be specified and if an end or objective be defined then there *must* be one best way of organizing the casual linkage of means to that end. Therefore, appropriate rational analysis should lead to its discovery, and hence such innovations as operations research, time and motion study, the assembly line, mass production and robotics.

Two world wars with their titanic deployment of men and materials, the development during and after World War II of general system theory, the manipulative findings of behaviorist psychology and group dynamics, the advent of the computer, and the modern philosophical movement of logical positivism have all served only to enhance and intensify the rationalist *Weltanschauung*.

Max Weber, for his part, is to be credited with the modern theory of bureaucracy and became to the office complex what Frederick Taylor was to the factory floor. In many ways he was a more accurate prophet of the political future than his near contemporary Karl Marx. His ideal-type theory clearly foreshadowed the growth of the Organizational State within which the ends of education have now to be devised.[14] Today administrators everywhere, in public or in private sectors of the economy, in public or private education, espouse the concepts that Weber formulated. A whole genre of social science literature attempts to reconcile the purity of Weberian theory with the imperfections of reality and practice.[15] In education the problem of bureaucracy has been acknowledged and analyzed in another massive body of literature.[16]

The fact is that bureaucracy, like its scientific godparent, *works*. The reality of life in the late twentieth century is an organizational environment of large and generally efficient bureaucratic systems: ministries, hospitals, police and armed forces, research institutes, schools, colleges, universities. The quality of life associated with this complex organizational society is, in turn, one of rational order, of supposedly impartial and impersonal equity, of extensive numeration and quantification and statistics.

Scientific and technological growth depend upon specialization, upon knowing more and more about less and less. This too is pragmatic —it *works*, it has proven to be successful. Our sci-tech bureaucratic culture has delivered increased command over nature. The organizational advances go hand in hand with the scientific-technological advances, as epitomized in NASA or the Atomic Energy Commission or, for that matter, the KGB. The ethical implications of these social trends toward complex organizational societies dominated by all-powerful state systems of governance and control, administered and entrenched via large bureaucracies rooted in a value ideology of positivistic rationalism are, to say the least, somewhat sinister. These systems deal by preference in quantitative rather than qualitative terms. In theory, the system owners or controllers, the elected representatives or trustees or directors, are supposed to solve value issues by choosing one quality over another quality, whereas numbers (the preferred modality of bureaucratic choice) are qualitatively indifferent —4 is in no way intrinsically superior or inferior to 5 or 105. The unit of policy analysis, the individual citizen, let us say, or the individual student in a multiversity, tends under bureaucratic influence to become a statistic abstracted of personal qualitites. This is indicated, for example, in the expression mass-man. This affinity for size and mass and for the depersonalizing arithmetic of large numbers, makes bureaucratic organization especially sinister because it can purport to be either ethically neutral (engaged only in rational quantitative calculus) or ethically equitable (since all human units are treated "equally"). And if this were not bad enough, such structures also provide, as we shall see, only too ample scope for the Machiavellian administrator who can pursue personal ends behind the facade of bureaucratic rationality.

There is yet a further cause for concern. The growth of statism or powerful government exercised through complex bureaucracy[17] affects all cultural development and especially the educational form of life. The ideology of statism, now universal in developed nations, conditions the public to believe in certain rights, such as the rights to health care, social welfare and education. Dependency upon the state for the provision of these rights, tends to render the individual malleable and amenable to government authority, that is, to administration in its largest sense. Max Weber foresaw the shape of things to come and how the chief instrumentality of the state, namely bureaucracy, would become ever more pervasive, intrusive and powerful. The quasi-profession of public service is now everywhere an established vested interest and the elementary political arithmetic and geometry of this administrative system[18] ensures the further propagation of a subtle ideology of statism. It establishes an ethos, a climate of values, a culture, and it is within this culture that educational leaders have to work, live, and determine their value commitments and their praxis.

Bureaupathology

Bureaucracy in its technical sense, as expounded in the Weberian ideal type,[19] is *a good thing*. It is rational, benevolent, efficient, reflective and fair. It connects means with ends according to the best principles of logic, science and jurisprudence. This ideal remains unimpeached *qua* ideal. Yet both layman and social scientist have other views. For the man in the street, bureaucracy is a *bad* thing. It seems to him to be irrational, malevolent, inefficient, ineffective and inequitable. For the social scientist it is a more problematic thing. The problem for social science is to explain why the empirical reality so often departs from or falls short of the ideal type. This has given rise to an extensive body of knowledge and research on the illnesses of bureaucracy, or bureaupathology.[20] Without being in any way exhaustive, one can illustrate the problem by considering briefly certain pathologies which have a particular moral or ethical import. For example: hierarchy, superficiality, dramaturgy, power, consensualism and characterology.[21] These six problems are chosen because they are universal and endemic in complex organizations. By and large, they tend to vary in severity in direct proportion to organizational size.

1. Hierarchy. This dilemma has been most cogently analyzed by Victor A. Thompson.[22] In essence, it means that as the tasks of the organization become more complex, technical and specialized the dependence of the non-specialist administrators upon specialist subordinates (professionals, technicians, technologists) increases while correspondingly their actual knowledge of the work of the organization diminishes. In one sense this is a straightforward and legitimate development of the principle of line and staff, but it becomes pathological when the line officers attempt to bolster their status and override personal insecurities about their competence by the irrational use of their veto power and by resort to a wide variety of dramaturgical techniques. When this happens pseudo-authority is used to compensate for technical ignorance. The consequences are deleterious to moral integrity as well as being organizationally dysfunctional.

In education the pathology can manifest with senior bureaucrats and school superintendents, for example, who have not done any classroom teaching for many years and perhaps no longer feel confident of being able to perform this, the most crucial function of educational expertise. Or college administrators may feel inadequate in any attempts to exert supervisory control over research, scholarly activity and teaching practices which are beyond their own disciplinary competence. How to *lead* where one has no understanding of what the followers *do?*

2. *Superficiality.* By extension from the hierarchical dilemma it can be shown that administrators are internally dependent in their policy making function upon information supplied by the specialists in the organization. That information is modulated by management gate-keepers in its upward passage through the hierarchy. As spans of control and spans of attention are both limited, it follows that at the highest levels there is at best an abstraction and loss of detail in the information base. This generalization and simplification of data is both inevitable and necessary in the Weberian theory, but at worst it can result in distortions and manipulations of the "reality" that the administrator is attempting to deal with. Moreover, the managerial side of administration/leadership is itself subject to intense fragmentation with consequent superficiality.[23]

> The scope for inauthenticity is increased while the opportunities for the exercise of true consideration and principle may wither under the steady impress of *ad hocism.* Meanwhile, however, the errant administrators will find in this superficiality neither guilt nor concern but rather comfort, for their very busy-ness serves to persuade them of their worth to the organization (are their diaries not crammed to capacity? their appointments bottlenecked?) which the organizations should reward by providing them with still more support staff and assistance. When this state becomes chronic the work ethic itself subserves and reinforces value pathology.[24]

In education we are familiar with the administrator-firefighter who rushes from problem to problem in an effort to put out fires. "School principals often have over a hundred human encounters in a day—make dozens of quick decisions."[25] Wolcott[26] compared the principal to a fireman responding to one emergency after another. And what intimacy has any university president with the actual operations of faculty whose disciplines are other than his own?

Busy-ness and superficiality are not necessarily dysfunctional per se but tend to become so at once when problems of value are raised. It is for this reason that the machinery of the law is designed to move at such a deliberate tempo. So too with the deliberative bodies (parliaments, senates, congresses) of the state. Bureaupathology can distort this aspect of the administrative/managerial distinction.

3. *Dramaturgy.* Since the social reality of large complex organizations, like that of society at large, is a socially constructed reality based on phenomenological perceptions,[27] the administrator cannot neglect his image. This image is a psycho-social artifact susceptible, as politically sophisticated citizens of modern media-dominated democracies are only too well aware, to the latest techniques of image manipulation. A pathology exists when dramaturgical performances[28] are substituted on a regular basis for authentic and substantive administrative work.

Educators are particularly concerned about their persona or image at every level from the classroom up. The especially political nature of public education may mean that from time to time substance may be subverted or replaced by an emptiness of style. There are indeed educational emperors aplenty who are wearing no clothes.

4. *The Problem of Power.* All administration depends on power. No power, no administration. "Power is the first term of the administrative lexicon."[29] Yet the status of power is ethically ambivalent. Dr. Johnson remarked that while the desire for power is deeply entwisted in human nature, it is to be pitied in others and despised in oneself. And while many are familiar with the first part of Lord Acton's dictum: "Power tends to corrupt and absolute power corrupts absolutely," not so many are familiar with the second part which asserts "Great men are almost always bad men." The problem of power can only be touched upon at this stage, but it can be noted that it is the subject matter of Machiavelli and earlier ancient classics such as the *arthasastra.*[30] To the extent that bureaucratic structures are conduits for the flow and generation of unauthorized as well as authorized power, they are susceptible of this pathology.

It would be naive to assume that educational administrators are somehow more immaculate than administrators in other fields when it comes to the acquisition, maintenance and enlargement of their organizational power bases. If they were this book might not need to be written.

5. *Consensualism.* Large bureaucratic organizations depend heavily on collegiate decision making and, as Barnard has shown, upon the support of lower levels of hierarchy. Moreover, organizations depend externally upon the political and economic support of outside groups (parents, voters, professional organizations) each of which makes value

claims and represents lobbies. There is a natural tendency, therefore, for administrators to seek to avoid offending any perceived interest group and, furthermore, to develop alliances or coalitions in support of policy. This is legitimate but can degenerate into the pathology of consensualism or "squeaky wheel" administration, wherein the administrator sacrifices value in the face of perceived pressures, responding only to the most vocal lobby, or seeking to extinguish complaints after the manner of the "fireman principle" referred to above. Whether or not the group values or consensus values are the *right* values is a question which we shall explore in depth in chapter 9.

6. *Characterology.* The easiest assumption to make, for followers and certainly for leaders, is that all leaders, all administrators, are honorable men or women. This indeed is the tacit assumption made by virtually all the contemporary textbooks in administration and organization theory. But there is no *prima facie* ground for this presumption and moreover, if the previous remarks about power pathology hold true, than the safer presumption would be that all administrators are *ipso facto* suspect! The Platonic dilemma, exhaustively analyzed in the *Republic,* is essentially that those who seek career advancement driven by ambition and the desire for success and power are precisely those who ought *not* to gain the office. By contrast, the Guardian, the morally elite leader, tends not to wish the burden of leadership office in the first place and is finally compelled to assume it only out of a sense of collective responsibility or duty.

It is quite remarkable that so much of the literature on administration and organization, including the canonical work of Max Weber in bureaucracy, makes little or no reference to the problem of the moral character of the incumbent of administrative office (Machiavelli for the negative and Chester Barnard for the positive are distinct exceptions).

The humane concerns of the educational project are particularly beguiling in causing us to lose sight of the problem of moral integrity in educational administration. It would be fallacious and it would be folly to allow our natural myths about great educators and our natural sentiments about the teaching profession to delude us into thinking that moral weaknses and corruption can be dissociated from educational administration. In other words, the problem of leader *character* has to be regarded as fundamental to any study of leadership.

If Not Bureaucracy Then What?

Given the above remarks, the reader might rightly interject at this point to ask, If the bureaucratic form of organization in despite of Weberian theory and in despite of its near-universal acceptance and entrenchment is subject to so many pathologies or ailments and is open to so much negative criticism, what is to be done? What alternative models, if any, exist?

The fullest answers to this question have been already given by Max Weber himself in his explication of the charismatic and paternal-traditional types of authority, with their corresponding modes of organization. At this point I shall only assert the possibility of a more congenial form for educational organization in the analog of the family. The family or extended family (clan, tribe, community, Gemeinschaft) is characterized by a tolerance and acceptance of diversity. No one is equal! It is understood that every member is unique and allowances of sympathy and compassion, quite irrelevant to the logical rational bureaucratic form, are continuously made and universally applied. No one is treated equally but everyone is treated equitably. The implications for leadership/administration are plain enough: the leader must get to know the followers, with insight if not with intimacy. He or she must cultivate some of the positive qualities of a parent: caring, responsibility, self-negation and self-sacrifice, concern for the future growth of charges, kindness and empathy. Such attributes can go far towards eliminating the illustrative bureaupathologies described above, even in a bureaucratic setting. And it may be noted in passing that even in the more tough-minded fields of administration associated with competitive industry, trade and commerce, such a familial emphasis has become increasingly popular, e.g., in the literature on Japanese management.[31] In education, of course, the epitome of this principle is to be found in the great collegial systems (Oxbridge) and private schools (Eton, Groton). Even bureaucratically organized public schools also seek through artificial devices such as "houses" and "homerooms" to achieve some measure of group belongingness and some acceptance of individual eccentricity. (Usually with markedly more success for the former than the latter.)

It should be stressed that a familial organization can only operate upon a tacit basis of faith. Faith that an underlying principle of justice or fairness or equity supports the surface structure of apparently differential treatment and partiality which might appear to the outsider to make some organization members more favored than others. From the standpoint of leadership this simply translates into a faith in the integrity or moral virtue of the administrator and this, then, is the chief component of that jargon concept, credibility. When credibility is added to the formal power base of the administrator, whether it be in bureaucratic, quasi-familial or authentically familiar forms of organization, the quality of life in that organization is felt by the followership to be more congenial and conducive to commitment. Whether there is a necessary linkage between warmth of human relations climate, organizational commitment, and productivity will be discussed in the next chapter. For now it seems reasonable to claim that since the peculiarity of educational organizations is an output occurring, in the last analysis, only within an individual human mind then that organizational climate[32] most compatible with the fullest psychological functioning is to be desired. This generalism does, of course, invoke a very large concept since mind may be interpreted to mean anything from neural programming at one extreme (behaviorism) to superrational (Spirit, soul, will) qualities at the other. So the distinction previously discussed (chapter 1) between training and education may be highly significant for the choice of best-fit educational organization. Other considerations in such a choice may also be the existing reality constraints in the form of political and economic considerations (enrollment, funding) or the inertial weight of past practice (tradition) and the defensible vested interests in established bureaucratic forms.

The Special Problems of Educational Leadership

A crucial difference between educational and other subsets of administration such as hospital, police, industry, trade and commerce is a lack of goal specificity. All of the latter know with some clarity what determines an effective organization and the evaluative criteria are built in through rational measures of health care, law and order, or profit. Balance sheets and statements of profit and loss can be drawn up and are overtly meaningful. In education, however, no such clarity of ends and means exists and, while financial statements of a sort can be ingeniously contrived, they are really meaningful only in showing discrepancies between budgetted and actual expenditures. To relate the budget itself to either the underlying educational philosophy or to ultimate educational outcomes is a task which is by no means overt or explicit and in general is of the utmost difficulty. To put it very bluntly, the educational enterprise does not always know where it is going, or what it is actually accomplishing, or even how to do what is supposed to be its primary task—the teaching-learning process. From an objective standpoint it is not at all clear to what extent teaching methodology is traditionalized ritual as opposed to scientific technology. Again, in contrast to other fields of administration, the actual raw material of education is intractably mysterious, for it is human nature itself. Thus educational administration is distinctively different and problematic on the three counts of ends, means, and evaluation.

Yet these very difficulties are the source of peculiar leadership opportunities: the opportunity to discover, clarify and defend the ends of education, to motivate towards those ends; the opportunity to discover means and invent process, since the prevalent state of pedagogic science permits rather than constrains; and the opportunity to create and establish morally grounded evaluation and legitimate it for all the participants in the great cooperative educational project. All of which means that educational leadership is especially difficult, especially challenging and especially moral.

The Central Problem

Another diagram may help to further clarify the essential nature of leadership/administration. Figure 2 re-orders the taxonomy of administration/management. The first stage in the dynamic and never-ending process of administration is deliberately labelled philosophy. Administration can be defined as philosophy-in-action.[33] Here philosophy means that the organizational values and *raison d'être* are articulated by top level administration. At this level, the *idea* of the organization is formulated and it is done by philosophical means: imagination, intuition, speculation, hypothesis, argument, dialectic, logic, rhetoric, value analysis and clarification. This ideational level of administration is then translated into the *plan*, the next phase in the emergent specificity of the idea. Next the plan must be entered into the political process of *persuasion*; it must be sold to those key individuals and organization members who ultimately control the resources necessary to realize the plan. The level of idea has now shifted to the level of *people*.

The whole process, still at this people level, now moves toward the mobilizing of the resources necessary to realization of the plan. Implicit in this phase, which has now become more managerial than administrative but is still within the realm of art and politics rather than science, is the motivation of the human resources of the organization to the collective purpose. When this has been accomplished, organizational means are brought to bear on ends and events occur not merely in the realms of *ideas* and *people* but also in the realm of things. The material order of the universe is changed in the direction of the organizational philosophy. These temporal events and their attendant resources need managing. Routines are established and adjusted. The quotidian work of the technical staff is organized. Finally, there is the necessity for monitoring, a phase which would include formal supervision, auditing, accounting, reporting, and evelation in the sense expounded most thoroughly by Stufflebeam *et al.*[34] The monitoring phase feeds back in the systems theory sense to the philosophy phase

FIGURE 2

Administration/Management

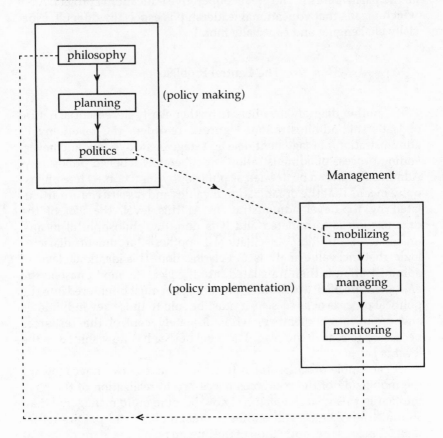

and the dynamic cycle of policy-making-administration/policy-implementation-management is completed. This total process can be conceived as the general field of leadership. It may be embodied in a single person or it may be partialled out into several specialities dependent on the complexity of the organization and its tasks. It is dynamic and recurrent and continuous with the cycle repeating and overlapping with the other cycles initiated at various points in the organizational history. The principle is always the same: a movement from ideas to things or events via the mediation of people. That is, the intellectual realm modifies the reality realm of the physical or natural world by human action. The central problem of administration, then, becomes the motivation of this action and, more precisely, since administration is always of a collective, it is to reconcile the self-interest of the individual organization member or client with the collective interest of the organization.

We shall explore this problem in the next chapter, but we can note at once that if the central task of education is the accomplishment of learning then the inculcation of motivation to learn must lie very close to the heart of educational leadership.

4

The Central Problem

In the last chapter we saw that the central problem of administration was one of reconciling two often divergent interests: those of the individual and those of the collectivity or organization. To make these interests converge upon the goals of the collectivity is to accomplish the core task of leadership. A classical statement of the dialectical tension was given by Getzels and Guba[1] in the diagram of Figure 1 below.

Here the organizational or administrative dimension is analyzed in terms of roles or job descriptions, each with its own set of behavioral (and attitudinal) expectations, while the personal or followership dimension is analyzed in terms of individual personality and its accompanying set of "needs dispositions." The conjuncture of these two dimensions, nomothetic and idiographic, results, through a vector resolution of forces, in "observed behavior." If one now substitutes "organization" for "social system" and "goals" for "observed behavior" one has a neat and nice depiction of the basic problem, i.e., reconciling the nomothetic and idiographic dimensions.

Another way of putting this is to assert that every formal organization is accompanied by an idiosyncratic *informal* organization, the knowledge and existence of which constitutes an onus upon the administrator to know the informal organization. Since no role incumbent ever perfectly fits the role expectations and always embodies individuality and idiosyncrasy, a large part of the art of leadership consists in the observation and judgment of character. A great leader is, to use Hitler's term, a *Menschenkenner*. One who grasps—instinctively, intuitively or otherwise—the motives of men.

From this it follows that the administrator's central and unending task is reconciliation. Reconciliation of the idiosyncratic individual to the organization and its goals as the internal task. Reconciliation of the organization to its environment (clientele, public, society, sub-culture and culture) as the external task. Since both dimensions, internal and external, are always in flux, we can define the administrative process as

FIGURE 1

Organizational Nomothetic Dimension

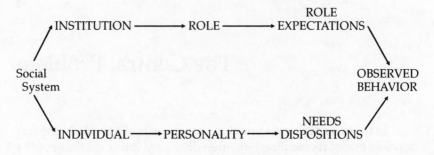

Personal Idiographic Dimension

the complex art of achieving organizational maintenance and growth in a field of conflicting and changing forces. This point is of sufficient importance to deserve a more extended and analytic treatment, one which will incorporate the notion of values. Figure 2 provides this expanded version. Within this scheme there are five levels or dimensions of value: V_1 through V_5. V_1 represents the personal value orientations brought by each organization member to the nomothetic role. V_2 represents the group value orientation of the immediate work group that the member belongs to (i.e., it incorporates the values of the informal organization). V_3 stands for the formal values of the organization as expressed in the overt and convert goals, policies and purposes of the organization as well as in the organizational culture.[2] V_4 refers to the values of the immeidate environment with which the organization is located (e.g., a formal bureaucracy may differ as between Greece and Turkey or a school as between urban and rural settings). Finally, the V_5 dimension is that of the explicit and implicit values of the overall or larger culture (nation, society, international community) as these are temporally affected by the *Zeitgeist,* or spirit-of-the-times. Schools and colleges were, for example, patently different in climate and administration as between, say, the countercultural convulsions of the 60s and the new-conservatism of the 80s.

Needless to say these dimensions, while analytically discrete, interact with each other in a systemic manner. A culture or a society is the totality of its organizations and these in turn are the totality of their idiographic human components. Culture both determines and is determined by individuals and so, for that matter, is an organization. For the leader, however, the central dimension of value is V_3. V_3 is the focus of

FIGURE 2

The Total Field of Leadership Behavior

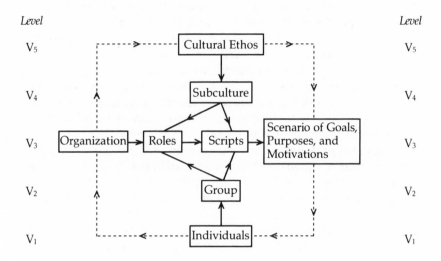

administration. It must predominate in the administrative consciousness. V_3 could be called the Formal-Nomothetic-Dramaturgical-Administrative Dimension. Formal because organizations exist as means towards formal ends. Nomothetic because formality demands structure and rules. Dramaturgical because the structure and its rules in turn create roles which have to be *acted out.*

Now because individual values, (V_1) are never perfectly aligned with the organizational role (V_2 and V_3) one is always to some extent constrained into playing a part and enacting a script which, although designed to achieve an organizational end, always subtly modulates in the direction of the actor's non-organizational desires. Of course, when a role performance is "bad" or too far out of the organizational "line," the actor must be dismissed or recast in another role. On the other hand, a fine performance is applauded and the actor is praised as being highly "committed". In *extremis,* he becomes the Organization Man as depicted by Whyte.[3]

This theatrical aspect of organizational life is overlooked in the Getzels-Guba model but has been clearly perceived and documented in the literature on administrative dramatizing, especially in the work of Victor Thompson[4] and in Goffmann's *The Presentation of Self in Everyday Life.* In educational administration the contributions of Gronn in Australia[5] and T. B. Greenfield in Canada are likewise notable, especially the latter's concern with facades and masks.[6] That there is a theatrical quality to organizational behavior in no way denies that there is also authentic engagement of the personality with the formal roles. What is important is that the bad fit between personality and role means that in formal organizations we are never truly or entirely ourselves. We exist to subserve organizational ends. And that very fact means that the Kantian ethical imperative: Never treat another human being as a means, is frustrated. At the very least such an ethic would have to be subjected to considerable re-interpretation. And hence, some might say, all leadership becomes a form of moral curiosity. Curiosity about followers' values, satisfaction, motives.

Despite such qualms, it remains true that the prime executive concern is the V_3 dimension, that which connects an organization with its purposes. It is the leader's responsibility to effect those aims and in doing so to somehow subordinate self to collectivity—that is, to the general will as that will manifests itself in organizational performance. And the leader must be aware that, in doing this, he or she is continually acting a part—the role of leader, the performance of which is public and will be continuously monitored by a variety of audiences, even when the script must be improvised and the scenarios are totally obscure. As we have already seen, obscurity of purpose is endemic in educational administration, and hence the demand for dramaturgical performance may be correspondingly enhanced.

In contrast to the administrator, the ordinary organization member encounters the V_3 dimensions indirectly, through workday interactions with those groups, formal or informal, that intervene between him and the executive level. In a corresponding manner, the prevalent V_5 ethic affects the organization not directly but indirectly, through some specific intervening subculture.

Taken together, the value dimensions V_1 through V_5 comprise the total field of executive action. While these levels overlap and subsume each other and interact in a variety of dynamic and contingent relationships, the administrator is always positioned, as it were, at the center of the vortex. From this position, the leader monitors outwardly the culture and sub-culture of the environment so as to make adaptive organizational responses, and monitors inwardly the informal organization and the individuals who compose the organization so as to elicit optimal performance and commitment.

The Basic Dialectic

This basic problem of reconciling personal and collective interests applies to all forms of governance. In educational administration the conflict is blurred and sometimes lost to sight through lack of definition. In commerce, trade, industry, politics and war the lines are more clearly drawn and hence the conflict is more obvious. In political theory as such the dialectic is between the individual and the state, or between anarchy and civil order, or between communism and capitalism, or between nature and human nature. Bloom sees the dialectic expressed in the conflicting philosophies of Locke and Rousseau: "The two outstanding intellectual types of our day represent these two teachings. The crisp, positive, efficient, no-nonsense economist is the Lockean; the deep brooding, somber psychoanalyst is the Rousseauan. In principle their positions are incompatible, but easygoing America provides them with a *modus vivendi*. Economists tell us how to make money; psychiatrists give us a place to spend it."[7] Or, from the leadership perspective: social science tells us how to manage our systems and industrial psychology tells us how to bandage the wounds.

In the history of administrative thought the dialectic has taken the form of a contest between two value orientations. The first of these, management science or scientific management stems from the classical work of Frederick W. Taylor.[8] The second derives from the equally classic work of the Hawthorne studies.[9] While a vast technical literature has since evolved about both these positions, the underlying models of man and basic presumptions about human nature can still be expressed, at the price of oversimplification, in the terms of McGregor's putative theories X and Y. Theory X postulates:

1. The average human being has an inherent dislike for work and will avoid it if he can.
2. Because of this most people must be coerced, controlled, directed, and threatened with punishment so that they will work toward the organization's goals.
3. The average human being prefers to be directed, prefers security, and avoids responsibility.

Theory Y postulates:

1. Physical work and mental work are as natural as play, if they are satisfying. *individual*
2. Man will exercise self-direction and self-control toward an organization's goals if he is committed to them.
3. Commitment is a function of rewards. The best rewards are satisfaction of ego and self-actualization.
4. The average person can learn to accept and seek responsibility. Avoidance of it and emphasis on security are learned and are not inherent characteristics.

5. Creativity, ingenuity, and imagination are widespread among people and do not occur only in a select few.[10]

That Theory Y contains five presumptions to X's three and that the first two are conditional may be taken by some to be suggestive of their author's biases or the temper of the times in which it was written. This does not, however, detract from the intrinsic dialectical oppositions. Nomothetic conformity is still set against idiographic deviance, only now the problem is cast in terms of values—in terms of our understanding of man. Implicitly the nomothetic dimension is allied to Theory X and its attendant rigors, while the more tender-minded Theory Y is proferred as the correct interpretation of the idiographic dimension and hence, tacitly, as *the* solution to the central problem of reconciliation.

Also implicit in McGregor's contrast is the notion that self-interest must either be coerced or seduced. Control can be effected through managerial technology—through time and quality control, accounting practice, supervisions—clinical and otherwise—all these are modes of coercion. Seduction can be effected through the manipulative techniques of group dynamics, human relations and personnel psychology, administrative manipulation of the "economy of incentives" and, on rarer occasions by the pervasion of charisma and what we shall later come to recognize as Type I values.

In educational administration a phenomenon of recent years has been the emergence of the large-scale industry of evaluation. Evaluation embraces both the corecive and the seductive aspects of the problem of self-interest. While initially intended to satisfy strident public and political demands for accountability in the baffling but ever more costly domain of public education, it later came to be subtly converted into a means of motivation or even, some would say, into a leader-substitute[12] This has come about through its own internal dialectic. The Theory X-based, "hard-nosed" assumptions of the initial evaluative effort, the thesis, were confronted by a Theory Y antithesis of teacher resistance and resentment generated in reaction to the initial evaluation attempts. The forces of group self-interest in the established system were in general sufficient to frustrate any simplistic efforts at evaluation and have led in time to an emergent synthesis whereby evaluators external to the evaluated system are obliged and compelled to enlist the cooperation of the evaluatees within the system. Hence, potential criticism is defused and transmitted into "participating leadership" and even "leader substitution". And, in terms of our dialectic, the pendulum is pushed in the direction of seduction and co-optation. That is to say, the evaluators are subverted by those whom they seek to evaluate and evaluation proceeds via obfuscation into a form of defense of the established order of interest. The basic dilemma only appears to have been resolved. In fact it remains.

Motivation and the Dialectic

The problem of reconciliation of divergent values and interests is typically recast in terms of motivation. In this mode of conception, the central leadership task is said to be that of motivating followers. But motivating is a neutral term and a vague one. It can range from brute coercion (the threat of dismissal, the promise of promotion) to the subtlest of psychological suggestions (the warm handshake, the raised eyebrow). Above all, it must be understood that motivation need not be rational. Appeals to reason and rational techniques such as salary and benefits may fail or pale before more powerful claims upon the emotions. These may include national or religious fervor, at one extreme, and sexual innuendo or incitements of *amour propre* at the other. In other words they may be slight, subtle and suggestive or strident, powerful and overt. Indeed the concept of motivation applies to the whole range and gamut of human affectivity. Moreover, the follower, even if committed to the organizational purpose (and hence not an obvious or immediate candidate for the leader's attempts at persuasion), is still only partially committed so long as his total personality is not identified with the organizational role. Motivation therefore is *always* less than complete. It is unstable and threatened by contingencies and conditions beyond the administrative field of action. Examples are legion. The teacher whose real life begins at 3 p.m. or when school closes for the summer; the student audience which heaves a collective sigh of relief when the lecture or seminar ends; the administrator who rejoices in travel, especially when it is outward bound.

Rousseau perceived this motivational discrepancy quite sharply at the political level of organization and suggested a radical remedy: the leader who would transform men's souls. Such a leader must

> ...so to speak change human nature, transform each individual, who by himself is a perfect and solitary whole, into a part of a greater whole from which that individual as it were gets his life and his being; weaken man's constitution to strengthen it; substitute a partial and moral existence for the physical and independent existence which we have all received from nature. He must, in a word, take man's own forces away from him in order to give him forces which are foreign to him and which he cannot use without

the help of others. The more the natural forces [idiographic] are dead and annihilated, the greater and more lasting are the acquired ones [nomothetic], thus the founding is solider and more perfect, such that if each citizen is nothing, can do nothing, except by all the others, and the force acquired by the whole is equal or superior to the sum of the natural forces of all the individuals, one can say the legislation [administration] is at the highest point of perfection it can attain. (*my parentheses*)[13]

While this sort of solution to the leadership problem can be considered naive, it is nevertheless a persistent theme in the literature and is still advocated by such sophisticated moderns as MacGregor Burns.[14] Indeed, this notion of the transformational leader is one to which we shall return often, especially in the discussion of charisma and the problems associated with Type I values (see chapter 5).

In some sense the dialectic can now be seen to be between reason and emotion, or between rationality, on the one hand, and the transrational or affective domains on the other. The forces of the former are aligned with those modern schools of administrative thought known as systems theory, Weberian bureaucracy, quantitative methods, behaviorism and scientific management.[15] The power of the latter is associated with movements such as human relations, human resources, democratic administrations, phenomenology, and philosophical humanism.[16]

While these opposing polarities represent the intellectual and ideological extremes, the center ground can be represented by the pragmatic realities of *de facto* organizational life. The dialectical struggle is dynamic and perennial: education as an administrative field aptly illustrates the tensions. Education is today conducted in increasingly complex bureaucratized systems, yet at the same time has obvious prepossessions with the idiosyncratic and humane aspects of maturation and social development (See chap 1.) The underlying philosophy adopted by the leader does, therefore, make a difference. If it is truly believed that the scientific method and rational empiricism are together necessary and sufficient for an understanding of human behavior—a view reinforced by the successes of service and technology in our culture—that is one thing. If, on the contrary, the emphasis is placed upon intractable constructs such as experience, value, consciousness, will, emotion, character and personality—all of which tend to frustrate the emergence of any hard, predictive theory—then that is another. The implications of each philosophical position for the leadership of organizations are contrary and contradictory. And any attempt at reconciliation or compromise can only be unstable, tentative and inconclusive in the basic conflict of ideas. Nevertheless, the executive must act and, consciously or unconsciously, this is done from some philosophical position and some concomitant theory of motivation. While the human element is always the point to which the philosophy of administration has to return, it must be admitted that contemporary value orientations in the developed world have been enormously influenced by the achievements of science and the overwhelming modern dependence on technology. Moon launchings and nuclear explosions, computerology, jet aircraft, television, the microchip, the control of disease—all intensify and deepen our appreciation of the rational, the logical, the empirical. And also, by extension, of the abstract and the general, as opposed to the concrete and particular. In a word, of the nomothetic over the idiographic. Science seeks laws and regularities (*nomos* in Greek); it seeks order and predictability; it is, at a deep psychological level, antipathetic to individuality and will. But science works and pays off. It passes the pragmatic test. It proves the adage that knowledge is power. At the V_5 cultural level this success, which rests on a philosophical distinction between fact and value about which much more will be said later, has resulted in value orientations of relativism, pluralism, hedonism, and pragmatism. These tacit public philosophies—the substance of conventional or orthodox wisdom— affect virtually every aspect of the educational leader's work. That work must be conducted in a society which is profoundly scientific, technical, rational-legal and, most simply, bureaucratic.[17] The emphasis upon rationalism in modern organizational life, the influences of Weberian-ideal type bureaucratic theory[18] and the development of modern systems theory[19] all go to endorse the latest neo-scientific management movement as it has developed over time from its Taylorian antecedents.[20]

But as always, action leads to reaction and the opposition to the new scientism seeks to form a new humanism. Speaking at the general (V_5) level, Sir Geoffrey Vickers in his book *Human Systems are Different* expresses this side of the dialogue:

The ideology deriving from the Enlightment which has dominated the West for two hundred years, has aspired to realize both liberty and equality, at first for the 'greatest number' and later for each and all. And it has hoped to do so by a self-regulating and self-exciting or self-stimulating process, powered by technology and directed by human 'reason'. In its pursuit of the doubtfully compatible goals of liberty and equality, this ideology has produced much that we should be sorry to forego; but the contemporary outcome is the reverse of what the nineteenth century expected. An ever more scientific world was never less controllable. A world dedicated to majority rules is increasingly run

by militant minorities. 'Free' individuals increasingly depend on
each other, are subject to increasing demands to share the commitments, accept the constraints and accord the trust required by
the multiplying systems and subsystems to which they belong
and on which they wholly depend. And these distribute their
favours and, still more their responsibilities, with the equality of a
battlefield....[21]

In this view, our V_5 culture intensifies V_1 frustrations and aggravates
the V_3 problem of administration. Indeed human systems are different.
And this because the human actor possesses an intractable element of
V_1 value which, while it may be averaged, masked, or authentically con-
cealed at the (V_2) group level of systems is still never entirely removable
from the administrative calculus. Hence the predictability and reliabil-
ity of natural science and technological mechanics can never be entirely
achieved. Hence, too, the existential nervousness about advanced
nuclear weapon systems. Despite all fail-safe guarantees, total security
remains elusive. Only, at best, can the ideal of complete control be
increasingly approximated. In the extreme administrative case we
would have a totalitarian logic where the values of the individual are
rendered almost completely irrelevant to the accomplishment of the
organizational task. From the ethical standpoint it then becomes just a
step towards that "banality of evil" described by Arendt and others in
reference to Adolf Eichmann and the death camps of Europe.[22] When
role conflict vanishes, when nomothetic and idiographic are thus reconciled, and when the individual comes to exist for the organization
rather than the converse, then that road lies open.

The persistent ill fit, on the other hand, between individual and
organization, the V_1-V_3 tension, assures the reality of continuing
dynamic adjustment of conflict. Conflict cannot be eliminated from
organizations; it is an essential, necessary and healthy part of their life.
The leader has not so much to solve value conflict as to resolve it,
continuously. Doing this cannot be a science, or a craft, but an art. Yet
curiously, what seems to go repeatedly unrecognized is that, as an art,
it must be grounded not merely in the social sciences (economics, psychology, social psychology, sociology) but also and above *all* in the
humanities (political science, listing history,[23] literature, the arts,
philosophy). "People skills" and political or human relations aptitudes
are now, of course, universally recognized as a desirable component of
administrative performance. To the extent that these attitudes can be
said to have any learnable intellectual substance, they are grounded in
both the social sciences and the humanities, but pre-eminently in the

latter since it is the function of the latter to interpret the former. Yet the curricula of schools of administration and management do not, by and large, reflect this reasoning. Grand exceptions exist. The British Civil Service in its highest reaches approves greatly of the generalist tradition whereby leaders are schooled in the classics or in such a curriculum as Oxford's P.P.E. (Philosophy, Political Science and Economics). The famous Japanese Matsushita School of Government and Management is another exception. Its curriculum is almost entirely humane and philosophical in scope and interest.[24] Other exceptions could be noted both in Europe and the U.S.A. but still the norm remains to the contrary. The myth that motivation can be scientifically comprehended (if not now, then surely later) persists and with it the corollary that the final synthesis, the resolution of the dialectic, is just around the corner. A convenient myth, perhaps, but still myth.

The Group and its Influence

The central problem—individual versus organization—can also be conceived more politically, i.e., in terms of democracy as opposed to monarchy or oligarchy; or even as liberalism versus authoritarianism. This cast of thought is clearly illustrated in the socio-psychological work of Kurt Lewin.[25] Lewin directed his attention to group behavior and the resulting social climates, which he characterized as authoritarian, democratic and laissez-faire. The implications drawn from these studies were preferential to democratic leadership, a conclusion perhaps not amiss given the times and the principal investigator's status as a refugee from Nazi Germany. Whether or not Lewin's conclusions were valid is unimportant in the face of the ideologized thrust given by this and similar work to the belief in democratic administration.[26] That is, it foreshadowed an emphasis in administration upon collegiality, collective decision making and consensus. The administrator is faced with the continuous task of seeking to build coalitions and must both discover and maintain consensus at all levels of the organizational hierarchy. The current vogue for Japanese management in business administration is a special case. While the ideas of this school of thought are certainly a function of the Japanese (V_5) value context, and while they may not translate well or "travel" to less homogeneous and hierarchical cultures, they nevertheless point to one pragmatic solution of the central problem: massive consensus. Long hours and days are spent and endless pains are taken by Japanese executives in the political task of consensus-building about goals and purposes at every level of organization, including the ultimate organization of the nation

state. When this is successful—and it is far from being always successful, even in Japan—it can be argued that this resolves once and for all
the central problem of commitment. Group and individual interest are
reconciled thereby. Yet the reconciliation may be more apparent then
real. And what is built may at once begin to erode.

Consensus is nevertheless sufficiently important to be treated as
a separate logical category of value; what we shall later analyze as the
Type IIB level of value discrimination (chpater 9). Group pressures at
the V_2 level effectively either seduce or coerce the individual within
that range of value that Barnard calls the zone of indifference.[27] In other
words, consensus only applies to that part of life within which an
individual identifies with his organizational role and within which he
accepts those values implicit in that particular organizational form of
life.[28]

Any ethical or moral critique of the above process must logically
be a critique of democracy and democratic values. Because of the heavy
impress of V_5 culture, because all political regimes educate in their own
image, and because that image in the West is currently egalitarian,
liberal, pluralist and relativistic, it is rare for such critique to be undertaken. It is rarer still for it to achieve publication. There is, as it were, a
solid consensus against any criticism of consensus. Especially is this so
in educational administration. In fact, it is only in the most recent times,
notably the work of Professor Bloom,[29] that any consistent critique
of democratic administration and democratic education has been
launched. The upshot of this is that educational administrators often
feel subservient to collective influence and opinion, especially as this
manifests itself politically and in the media. Nevertheless, as the next
section reveals, their power is greater than they might think.

Administrative Power(V_3)

Let us now consider the central problem from the differing standpoints of the leadership (V_3) and the followership (V_2, V_1). Modern
organization theory and social psychology have constituted major
insights for each of these standpoints. From the V_3 aspect we must
especially take into account the work of Stanley Milgram. This derives
essentially from the now famous, but to some infamous, series of experiments conducted in the 1950s and known generally as the Milgram
studies.[30] For ethicists it is of interest to note that these experiments
were conceived with the intent of proving that the Nazi death camp
was an organizational phenomenon which could never have occurred
in a liberal democracy such as the United States. Of interest, too, is the
fact that, for purely ethical reasons (conventional norms having shifted

during the 1960s), these experiments cannot now be replicated or verified. Professional standards now prohibit the manipulation of naive subjects in psychology, if not in administration proper.

In the experiments themselves, naive subjects were required to administer supposed electric shocks to a supposed victim upon the commands of various authorities. The shocks could reach massive proportions, sufficient, in the mind of the naive subject, to cause grievous bodily harm or even death. The victim was a confederate of the experimenters. The results seemed to show conclusively that there was a powerful predisposition to obey a superior's commands, even if those commands violated the values of the subordinate and caused him considerable pain and distress. In other words, the propensity to obedience was much greater than had been imagined, so great, in fact, that atrocities could occur under any system of government, as later historical events such as the My Lai incident seemed to confirm. That is, administrators had a most significant power base and the overriding of ordinary morals scruples could easily be accomplished in an organizational context. The contest need not be a military one. The findings apply to all subsets of administration, including educational administration.

It is important, of course, not to be facile in interpreting these complex experiments. Evidence was also adduced of principled behavior and the existence of "conscience". Many of the naive subjects who obeyed fully, even while believing they were seriously threatening another human's life, expressed much affective misgiving and distress in the debriefing sessions. Nevertheless, the findings were unexpected and ominous and they led the researcher to postulate the concept of an *"agentic state"*. This is a psychological set or condition into which a subordinate rapidly falls when placed in a context of formal organization. It is a condition of ready obedience and willingness to be commanded. It can exist in mild, moderate, or extreme forms, such as the totalitarian or military ideal, but it is always present from the outset. All that is required to produce it is that the trappings, symbols and attitudes of authority and office be appropriately presented, in other words, that the dramatizing of roles be properly played out. Thus, we fall easily into the agentic state in the doctor's or the lawyer's office or in the presence of uniformed police or customs officers.

Milgram postulated that obedience to authority performs an evolutionary function; it promotes survival. Submissiveness to authority has bio-ethical merit. In war or conditions of social threat the phenomena intensifies, but, even in the most liberal of social circumstances, there is a constraint which makes it easier to obey than disobey. In a word, obedience is the line of least resistance; hence, the administrator has at his service the means for designing authority systems which can override many if not all of V_1 scruples, preferences and inclinations. The zone of indifference or acceptance is always larger than the leader may think. The leader may well have more power than he imagines.

Scott and Hart[31] have also analyzed what they call the organizational imperative. This imperative proposes that (1) "Whatever is good for the individual can only come from the modern organization" and consequently (2) "All behaviour must enhance the health of such organizations." Therefore, the organizational ethic dictates that (a) the task of administration is to maximize efficiency, defined as the ratio of output to input, (b) administrators owe primary loyalty to the organizational imperative and, (c) administrators must be expedient and must focus on short-term reality to the exclusion of long-term idealisms. Taken together this value analysis by Scott and Hart suggests a strong and increasing domination of organizational or V_3 values over those of the individual and the group. The power of the organization, according to this, approaches near-hegemony and it is the administrator who has command of that power.

Follower Power (V_1)

The previous section has shown that the executive power of the leader is perhaps considerably more than he or she might have imagined. This may be especially true in those complex administrative arenas of higher education where the diffusion of power and influence combined with the collegial ethos may seem at times to render any sort of leadership impotent. There is a dialectic at work here. Power in one sense always rests ultimately with the formal legal structure. Power in another sense always rests ultimately with the individual components of that structure. They can quit, walk away, or sabotage the organization, while conversely the law can force them to carry out their functions and their roles. Soldiers, for example, can be forced to fight, but they can also desert and mutiny. So a dialectic of power is always present between the apex and the base of structure—that is, between leaders and administrators, on the one hand, and the membership or followership on the other.

Barnard, in his classic *The Functions of the Executive,* was among the first to recognize formally that *in potentia* at least, the ultimate power rested with the followership. The pressure to obey may be great indeed but in the final analysis the subordinate can always withhold obedience, covertly if not overtly. The truth of this, in turn, seems to rest on an irreducible antagonism between individual and organization. This is the essence of the research conducted by Argyris; his extensive studies lead him to conclude that a healthy personality cannot achieve a perfect fit with the requirements of formal organization:

> ... this inevitable incongruency increases as (1) the employees are of increasing maturity, (2) as the formal structure ... is made more clear-cut and logically tight ... (3) as one goes down the line of command, and (4) as the job became more and more mechanized....[32]

Argyris also delineates some of the patterns of reaction to this value conflict: quitting, seeking promotion, resorting to apathy or sabotage, featherbedding, absenteeism and so on. In short, it may be as simple as this, that there is always something constraining about formal organization. We can never become totally committed to any institution. Wills, however developed or underdeveloped, enter into conflict. Hell, as Sartre says, is "other people." Especially, we might add, when they are in power relationships over us. So long as the flame of individual will is not extinguished (a possibility which even Hitler admitted as beyond the reach of any leader), the administrator is obliged to deal with what, from the organizational standpoint, can be conceived of as a sort of moral slack, a deficit of commitment.

The means to reduce this deficit are coercion or persuasion. In fact, they involve the whole range of human power interactions: argument, flattery, guile, guilt, exhortation, example, charisma, symbol, bribery, myth, force, domination, manipulation, inspiration, energy, malice, love—the whole gambit of techniques that have been learned over the long history of administration and which each succeeding generation of leaders must either relearn or else practice instinctively. The follower not only has power. He has ultimate power.

Culture Power (V_{2-5})

In addition to the powers of the leader, the group, and the individual, there is also, surrounding the organization and permeating it, an influence upon values and desires which can be termed cultural. It can manifest or originate at any value level from V_2 to V_5. Its effect, though real, is often sbuliminal or unconscious; below the level of awareness in the same way that fish are unconscious of the sea in which they swim—it comes with the territory and with the role. The mere fact of being a professional, for example, means that one is subject to a set of norms which are not merely expectations of behavior but also ways of perceiving and evaluating.These norms are part of the induction and initiation processes of professionalism. These processes may give the recognized professional a certain power of status and expertise but they also subject him to the power of his professional culture.

In this example, the specific organization is transcended for the larger community of the profession, but it is equally true that organizations create their own influential and powerful cultures. The value orientations of these cultures permit some degrees of freedom. The individual may choose to be variant or deviant from the culture, but within limits. Military and ecclesiastical limits may be more constraining than those of educational organizations, but not necessarily so. Consider the elite schools of the world and their capacity for graduating students who carry the impress of their school culture visibly and permanently into their later lives. Less so, but likewise, even bank tellers and salesclerks, as much as incoming teachers and faculty members, must discover and abide by "the way we do things here".

Organizational culture has been defined by Schein as "a pattern of basic assumptions—invented, discovered, or developed by a given group as it learns to cope with its problems of external adaptation and internal integration—that has worked well enough to be considered valid and, therefore, to be taught to new members as the correct way to perceive, think, and feel in relation to those problems."[33] It follows that culture is essentially conservative. It serves to integrate, maintain, and to adapt in the interests of the maintenance and growth of a given set of values. This does not mean that it is impervious to change, only resistant to it. A culture that is rigid dies, as does one that is over-flexible. The former eventually breaks while the latter never takes on form.

Within the growth and change parameters of a viable culture the role of the leader is crucial. The leader can create new culture and reinforce the old. In this there are two aspects: the outer and the inner. The outer aspect calls for monitoring, investigation, searching and observation of the various subcultures within the organization. This includes investigating the shifting patterns of informal organization; in other words, intelligence gathering. It is accomplished as much by simply looking and listening as by Peters and Waterman's "management by walking around."[34] It also embraces a steady monitoring of the external cultural environment and all those political, social and media interactions that affect the organization in any way.

The inner aspect refers to a parallel searching, monitoring, investigation and observation of the leader's own values, internal conflicts, philosophy and ideology. The question always to be asked is "Where do I stand?", "What does this really mean to me?"

The combination of these two leadership aspects confirms the maxim that knowledge is power and, in effect, at least with respect to organizational culture, places the leader in a power position superior to that of the followership. It lies at the base of the mystery of charisma. Other-direction is transcended by inner-direction and, when this charisma is harnessed to orgainzed mission, an organizational culture is born.

A word needs to be said here about the non-organizational culture: the V_5 and V_4 impress that is beyond the leader's direct control. A school in Lebanon is not the same as a school with identical physical characteristics in Israel. Even rigidly uniform MacDonald's hamburger franchises vary distinctly, even between close geographical locations. These psycho-social differences reflect differences in value orientation. The orientation in the larger culture (V_5) changes slowly and indiscernibly across the decades, even though the *Zeitgeist* of the 1980s is so patently different from that of the 1960s or the 1930s. The movement of ethos is beyond the leader's intervention or control. What he or she can do, however, is monitor. The leader can and must try to sense the spirit of the times and the direction of trends, and fulfill a duty to match organizational culture with the larger culture that surrounds and sustains it. If the leader is perceptive enough and skilled enough the organization may be brought to the growing edge. Or, conversely, one may feel a *moral* duty to resist the perceived trends—consider, for example, the problem facing church leadership over the cultural issue of ordaining homosexual ministers. This culture modulates V_3 administrative power. It can enhance or diminish it and, *in extremis,* make or break the administrator. And the organization likewise; captain and ship may go down together.

The play of cultural forces from above and from below, from without and from within, compound the central problem of administration. An administrator, for example, may be constrained to become what used to be called an "organization man"[35] while, at the same time, the culture of private life dictates individualism, hedonism, and "self actualization". Personally, as well as for others, the leader must then reconcile these two sets of interests. Such reconciliation entails interpersonal and intrapersonal conflict. This means stress and perhaps that is why administrators lay claim to so great a share of the organizational reward system.

The practical implications for leadership are fourfold. Four sets of value knowledge and experience are required. These are: (1) knowledge of the task or mission (the aims, ends, goals, objectives, purposes, philosophy and policy of the organization) i.e., V_3; (2) knowledge of the situation within which that task must be accomplished, i.e. V_4 and V_5, the cultural context; (3) knowledge of the subordinate and peer personnel who have to achieve the mission and carry out the task, i.e., V_2, the followership and (4) self-knowledge on the part of the leader, reflective scrutiny, value audit and confirmation, i.e., V_1.

Of these four knowledge bases, the first two; task and situation, represent the external or objective side of things. Facts are important here for they represent the "reality constraints". The sum of the facts constitutes paramount reality.[36] This forms the context and basis for the values which then enter into and determine the action. If the horse needs a nail in his shoe or the philosopher has a toothache then the battle may be lost or the insight fail to be discovered. But the business of warfare and philosophy rest ultimately on values.

The second two knowledge bases; of the followership and of one-self, represent the internal or subjective side of leadership. Here the methodology is observational, intuitive, experimental. One learns to become a *Menschenkenner*—a knower of men—by people study, by a special kind of consciousness acquired in interaction with them, and by reflection upon this experience.

Towards a Philosophic Solution

The central problem can also be considered as the philosophical problem of selfishness. That is, the problem of human desire. Desire is at the root of motivations. Circumstances constrain us, frustrate our ends or provide the means to achieve ends in despite of frustration; but the ends are born out of desires. Values are concepts of the desirable, and because administration is essentially motivational and valuational, it is intrinsically philosophical. It is squarely in the realm of morality. One could say that all leaders are philosophers and educators (which is not at all to say that they are any good at these things) because they are engaged, commonly or otherwise, in the education of desire—in persuasion about ends and the conversion of means into ends.

The spectrum of administrative philosophy is very large; it begins in the dirt and ends in the stars. It aspires to the highest ideals of the species, builds nations and empires, seeks honor, glory and posterity and at the same time encompasses all the flaws and defects that the human condition is heir to, including malevolence, hatred, envy, greed, lust and rage. Even its greatest achievements are limited by some measure of perversity and corruption, yet always, somehow, it places the whole above the part, the greater against the lesser interest, the nomothetic over the idiographic, ends in advance of means. Great organizations are always in some sense ideological or educational; they seek to change their members, make them conform to their own ideal, subscribe to their culture. So leaders become educators, educators become leaders, and the moral burden is inescapable.

Educational administration is itself a moral activity, as we have already shown. Educational organizations are also invested, it will be remembered, with the problem of the hidden or "moral" curriculum. This phenomenon is very akin to what theorists in general call organizational climate. When the principal of a school is a mere factotum and moral cipher, when the superintendent of a school district is a philistine, when an academic vice-president is a machiavellian careerist, when a university president capitulates to minority demands out of fear of adverse public relations, it follows that the morale and the moral character of their respective organizations will be affected. A new perception of the way things really are is then transmitted and the price may be high in terms of increased cynicism, scepticism, negativity, alienation and hedonistic self-seeking on the part of students and faculty alike—and conversely when positive signals are transmitted.

Moral leadership is achieved when the administration maintains a productive tension between philosophy and action. Effective leaders employ philosophy to curb the natural tendency of organizational members to overemphasize individual "spiritedness", or emphasis on self:

> Executive responsibility, then, is that capacity of leaders by which, reflecting attitudes, ideals, hopes, derived largely from without themselves, they are compelled to bind the wills of men to the accomplishment of purposes beyond their immediate ends, beyond their times.[37]

Note the word "largely" in the above quotation. It is important. It reveals Barnard's concern with what we have analyzed above as followership power and culture power. But it also points to the residue of value located within the leader himself. Barnard's classic statement is reiterated by Burns with his concept of "transformational leadership" which is, he says, "more concerned with end-values such as liberty, justice, equality" and is such that "people can be lifted into their better selves."[38]

The solution of the central problem must them be sought first in the domain of philosophy. What we are seeking is, in fact, a theory or philosophy of selfishness such that it might be applicable to the field of administrative action, of leadership. Such a theory might encompass what we could call the morality of selfishness as well as the morality of honor. It would have to allow for such psychological aspects as the span of affective control, "distancing", compartmentalization, and ruthlessness. Above all, it must clarify our notions of responsibility, morality, ethics and values. To these topics, therefore, we next turn in the following chapters.

III
The Moral Art

5

Value Theory

All of the discussion to this point has shown one thing: that administration or leadership in its fullest sense is more concerned with values than with facts. The central problem itself is a value problem. But what's value? What are values? How do they differ from facts? Can one have a fact without a concomitant value? Can we be objectively neutral or "value free"? Can one derive values from facts? These are all questions that the serious leader must explore.

Let us begin with the distinction between values and facts. This is essential to our understanding. We should not, however, be over-concerned with definitions at this point. For practical preliminary purposes we can take values to be *"concepts of the desirable"* and facts to be, as Wittgenstein once said, "all that is the case." The first thing to note is that for any given state of affairs the facts can *never* be in conflict while the values, assuming that there are more than one set, are *always* in conflict. This difference is fundamental. It comes about because facts pertain to the objective world of nature and science. They are by definition true; a false fact is an oxymoron. Moreover, in the Aristotelian West at least, this truth is universal. A thing is either A or not A; it either is or it isn't, that is how the world is made up. It is worth remarking that this logic, which is at the foundation of Western science and materialism, has in our time received considerable reinforcement through the electronic revolution. A computer, after all, is merely a complex of on-off, either-or, is or isn't switches.

But the world of value is altogether different. If the world of fact has any value at all it is only that which is imputed to it, superimposed upon it, by a subjective consciousness. By a mind. The world as it is experienced through the mind of an observer appears to be colored with values, but the world in its factional essence is void of value—without beauty or ugliness, right or wrong, good or bad. To paraphrase Plato, a thing is not valued because it is good, it is good because it is valued. Man is the esteeming or valuing animal. Though he is not alone; other animals value. As we shall see, they distinguish between what is "good" and "bad" for them, but man appears to be the only animal capable of making the right/wrong kinds of valuations. He is, as Nietzsche called him, "the beast with red cheeks." The only life-form capable of shame.

Because of the radical difference between fact and value, it is both possible and likely for two observers to attribute two divergent values or sets of values to the same piece of objectivity or fact. Indeed they must do so, if only for the simple reason that everyone experiences the world from a different angle. No one can occupy the same life-space as another. The world comes up differently each time for each person. Therefore, in some very fundamental sense values are always in conflict.

The administrator need not, of course, take this to the extreme of Sartre's claim that "Hell is other people." Yet the leader should note that the bulk of collective behavior, political or social or organizational, is devoted to and dependent upon the establishment of some sort of *modus vivendi* or working resolution of value conflict. An organization is, strictly speaking, an arrangement for conflict management through the device of superordinate or overriding goals.

Now let us turn to the question, Can one derive a value from a fact? It would certainly be useful if we could, for then the administrator need simply be concerned with the facts of the case. Can one, for example, go along with the following?

> "She is a teacher of 7-year olds in our local school; therefore she should teach them to read" is, for me, a true statement irrespective of the curricular context in which she works. This is not to assert there can be no distinction between fact and value, but it is to assert that *value statements can be and are derived from factual statements.*" *(my italics)*[1]

But Holmes, the author of this quotation, is wrong. He is committing what is technically called the naturalistic fallacy. The value premises in his example are there prior to the definition of teacher; they are *a priori* not *a posteriori* and they are derived from a set of values about the nature of education and teaching. Once the values are set then one can, of course, appear to derive values from the value-loaded fact, but to do so is merely trivial or vacuous; like saying a knife is good because it is sharp and meets the preordained instrumental criteria of the concept "knife". Moreover, since world views differ, since they shift continuously over time, since they are learned through social conditioning, and since they are also to a degree matters of personal choice or preference then it follows that values are relative and not absolute. The concept "teacher" like the concept "knife" carries different value connotations from culture to culture and from time to time.

Facts, on the other hand, are absolute within the system of natural science. At least to the level where quantum mechanics and the principle of uncertainty do not apply.

There is, thus, not only a Great Divide between value and fact, but also a division of equivalent proportion between the absolute and the relative. With these distinctions made we can now proceed to consider how they have affected administrative thought and the concept of leadership.

Traditional and Classical Notions

The most fundamental and ancient question in administrative philosophy can be phrased radically as follows: Ought a leader to be honorable or ruthless? Moral or amoral? To this can be added a further, more modern interpretation of the question: Ought an administrator to be committed or neutral? Passionate or professional? Throughout history the pendulum has swung between these poles of good and evil, passing on its way through the deadpoint of impartial neutrality.

Plato advocated that there be a special breed of leader, the Guardians, exponents of the Good who would administer safely and wisely the perfect state, the *Republic*. Such leaders would be *intrinsically* superior to their subordinates by virtue of the fact that they had had a glimpse, however fleeting, of the Form of the Good, the ultimate and absolute *Ideal*. A concept which might also be captured in such terminology as Good, Absolute, Infinite, Transcendental. This authenticating vision was to be achieved through discipline. The Guardians were to be men of experience and mature years who had overcome the ordinary desires for success, power and sensual pleasure. Single and celibate, they were to live simply and without luxury. Their burdens of responsibility were assumed, not because they wanted the rewards and perquisites of office, but precisely because they did not. These were not ordinary men but philosophers. With them the Republic could be born. Without them it could not.

This notion of aristocracy or meritocracy—the elitism of the good —did not die with Plato. It may seem now outrageously romantic or idealistic, yet the appeal of this vision has never entirely faded. Its lineaments are displayed in the Society of Jesus, the Communist party as the vanguard of the proletariat, and elite leadership schools throughout the world to the present day. The common factor in all these modern versions of Platonism is that of concern with an ethic, a moral engagement or commitment which both commands sacrifice from its adherents and endows them with a sense of superiority. It is fair to say that there is a religious or mythical quality to this tradition. Underlying it is some vision of the good, whether that be the perfect harmony of the Republic, the Utopian Workers' State, or the New Order envisioned by Nazi romantics. The mythology provides the value dynamic for the movement and is essentially transrational in character. In other words, this type of leadership goes *beyond* reason.

Diametrically opposed to this is the tradition of the leader as a man of power. Such a man is governed by an ethic of success. He is totally ruthless in the pursuit of this end, in the acquisition, maintenance and expansion of his power. All means justify his ends and he is strong, bold, amoral—beyond good or evil in the conventional sense. He is typified by Machiavelli's *Prince,* but the ancestry of this school of administrative thought can be traced back to the earliest mists of time as, for example, in the Sanskrit *arthasastra.* Perhaps because of its reality base, as opposed to Platonic ideality, a sizable literature exists in the genre known variously as *Realpolitik* or *Fuerstenspiegel*—a "mirror for princes". The lure of "success" is itself powerful. Practical formulae for the achievement of success have always had a certain appeal. History and the arts record many anecdotes of the more Byzantine modes of administrative life. In general, normal ethics and morals are simply jettisoned or abandoned, although careful pains may be taken by the leader to disguise this fact from the followers, who themselves presumably subscribe, at least overtly, to such morality. Treachery, trickery, guile, corruption all have their instrumental place in this scheme of things. In ancient China this sometimes secret doctrine or path was known as "School of Thick Face, Black Heart" while in India it was known as the *Arthasastra,* or doctrine of Success. Study of these techniques and the desire to become an adept could not of course be overt. Conventional institutions of learning would be obliged to proscribe such teachings. Nevertheless, the desire for power and success, for wealth and fame at any price is probably as widespread in human nature today as it was at any other period of history and, consequently, the appeal of this ethos means that such doctrines persist in practice and praxis, however much they may be deplored by departments of administration, government, political science, and philosophy. Even at the intellectual level, however, a counter-Platonic stream of thought persists and is well understood in the practical realm. Graduate students have always intrigued me, for example, by the liveliness of their interest upon first encountering *The Prince.* And the modern philosopher Nietzsche, though little read and still less understood by administrators in general, has provided for some a trans-moral and transrational justification for the ethic of ruthlessness and the strong-man type of leader, the man who goes beyond the values of the herd to create his own world of value. Shakespeare's Richard III, Othello's lieutenant Iago, and Dostoevski's Grand Inquisitor are literary images of the type. And here, perhaps, we can say that this type of leadership also goes *beyond* reason, but in a direction anitithetical to that of Plato.

Other alternatives exist in the history of administrative thought. The administrative leader need be neither morally subversive nor morally sublime, but may simply take value directions from convention or tradition. Or the leader may seek to avoid philosophical and value issues altogether by becoming a technician, a factotum, a manager. By retreating to managerialism[2] he may seek a sort of disengagement or divorce from the value implications of the role and become a mere conduit for the flow of moral or immoral action. But in the end this proves vain, if only because personality can never be entirely expunged from role performance. Even that epitome of Max Weber's ideal type bureaucracy, the career civil servant void of all political will and totally at the behest of political masters, concerned solely with rational analysis and the delivery of dispassionate advice, even this example proves upon inspection to be a fiction and a myth.

The problem returns to this: An administrator, any administrator, is faced with value choices. To govern is to choose. One can accept or not accept the value dictates imposed by the particular organizational culture in which one works. One can aspire to or can disdain any of a number of systems of "ethics" ranging from workaholism to neo-Confucianism. One can allow, or not allow, one's leadership to be swayed by values deriving from hedonism, ambition or careerism, or by the prejudices and affinities one has for colleagues and peers. Each day and each hour provides the occasion for value judgments, and each choice has a determining effect on the value options for the future.

Since values are ultimately inescapable, upon what grounds then can, or should, one choose? What values are the *right* values? How are the values of the case before us to be ordered? How to achieve that degree of certainty which can imbue us with a sense of philosophical satisfaction and psychological security?

It must be conceded at the outset that all the classical and traditional theories of value fail to resolve these questions. The answers which ethics delivers are in the final analysis dogmatic. The business of ethics is a sort of preaching. Perhaps this explains why codes of ethics are, in practice, about as convincing and efficacious as are preachments and moral exhortations in general, whether delivered from the pulpit, the parade ground, the political rostrum or the chief executive's chair.

Let us therefore take a different approach. Let us consider the problem of *value itself.*

The Nature of Value

Value Terminology

To disentangle, so far as we can, value from fact is a step forward in our understanding, but we must now cope with another order of linguistic confusion. This stems both from common sense and from the facts and theories of psychology. An example is provided by the term"needs". Maslow, the great psychological value theorist, rarely wrote of values as such, but preferred instead to talk about needs. What are needs and how are they to be distinguished from, say, wants or desires?

The idea behind need is that of a discrepancy or undesirable imbalance in a state of affairs. Needs imply tension and disequilibrium and provide a dynamic for rectifying action. We shall take needs and the cognate terms "desire" or "wants" as being indicators of some state of individual or group deficiency or shortfall, with a consequent potential or propensity for remedial action. As such, they are *sources* of value.

Needs, wants and desires are also related to the concept of motive. The idea behind motivated behavior is usually that there is for the motivated actor some kind of end-in-view. The trouble with this interpretation is that the end may not be "in view". It may be semiconscious or even unconscious. The impulse to action may be subliminal; psychological language contains such concepts as "drives" and "drive states" about which there is much contention and inconclusive experimentation. For our purposes, let us accept motives as either conscious reasons or unconscious drives, or some combination of both, which are a source of value. I may be fully aware, partially aware, or totally unaware of my motives for action, but the fact that I myself or other observers can pass value judgments upon those motives is sufficient to show that value is something other than motives, desires, wants or needs.

Motives, then, have this push-pull correlation with consciousness and the faculty of reason. To be completely unmotivated is not to exist as a sentient being. To be fully aware of all our motives would be to be supersentient. And to approve of them all would be superhuman. Motives existing in the depths of the psyche as dark forces of the id or fully exposed in the light of day as validated and justified reasons are also correlated with the phenomenon of attitude.

I wish to define attitudes as surface phenomena, predispositions to act or respond to stimuli in relatively stable or persistent ways. As

FIGURE 1

Schema of Value-related Terms

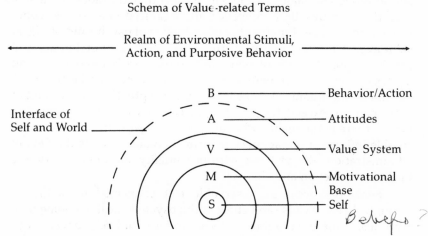

motives provide a source of value, so value is a source of attitudes. Attitudes are manifestations of values at the interface of skin and world. The world demands attention in a great variety of ways. How we attend is a function of our attitudes. And attitudes are measurable facts in the world. If we take the simplest biological organism we may, by observation, reduce and classify the number of attitudes to two or three: fight, flight, or freeze. For the complex human organism, the attitudes may be legion because this level of organic complexity is linguistic, engages continuously in language games (one of which is called administration) and expresses its attitudes in language categories, some of which are referred to as opinions. Thus, polls assess collective attitudes and individuals are categorized as open-minded or close-minded, conservative, radical, authoritarian, permissive, innovative and so *ad psychologium nauseamque infinitum.*

Let us note, however, the arithmetic of this line of reasoning. First, there is the unitary self (we avoid the complexity of split and multiple personalities described in psychoanalytic literature). Next, a very few basic motives: perhaps a bare will to survive or the Freudian dualism of eros and thanatos, an urge to life counter-balanced by a wish for surcease. At a more surface level, but still interior and closely related to the integration of the self, the deep-seated motives are manifested in a system of values. These value complexes or value orientations depend uon their holder's circumstances, biography and culture. They may be unconscious and in logical contradiction as, for example, when kindness and honesty are openly (consciously) expressed, but the ruthless and dishonest acquisition of wealth and success is secretly or subliminally admired. The values are more in number than the motives, but less than the attitudes. Both, however, are organized more or less cohesively into systems. Emergent at the interface of psyche and world, at skin-level as it were, are the attitudes, expressions of preference and predispositions to act in response to the countless issues of living and life style. They are commensurable in so far as they can be observed, classified and organized so as to make conceptual sense. In number they logically exceed the underlying values which they represent. Lastly, there is the realm of behavior and action with its incommensurable infinity of possibilities. It is this domain which is the field of administration, always tense with potentiality and opportunity, the birthplace of action and change.

Behaviors occur as observable fact connected by inference through chains of cause and effect to the psychological phenomena of attitudes, value orientations, values, motives, and self-concept. The scheme described above is shown diagrammatically in Figure 1. The figure is not intended to be dogmatic or definite. It does not specify, for example, the locus or function of *will* about which much more shall be said later, nor does it explain how the several components are articulated. But it is pragmatically useful as a descriptive and explicatory device for the argument which follows. It postulates a continuum, at one end of which are private (but culturally conditioned) value phenomena, perhaps intensely private and inaccessible to public verification. At the other end of the continuum are purposive behaviors and strivings taking place in an observable, public, collective realm in which motives can be spelled out linguistically as goals and collective purposes and in which values can be expressed verbally as ideas, *summa boni*, social norms and cultural standards. Such values may occasionally be objectified into systems of law, codes of ethics, systematized philosophies and ideologies. Between these extremes lie the gamut of attitudes, opinions, preferences. The continuum is dynamic through the action of modulating feedbacks and feedforwards. From its ground in individual consciousness to its revelation in the public play of sensory data, the universe is intentional and teleological.

A Value Model

I now wish to present an analytical model of the value concept which I believe has some merit in helping us to chart our way across the seas of value confusion. It will also enable us to classify values and eventually establish some bases for the resolution of value conflicts. The model is given in Figure 2.

FIGURE 2

Analytical Model of the Value Concept

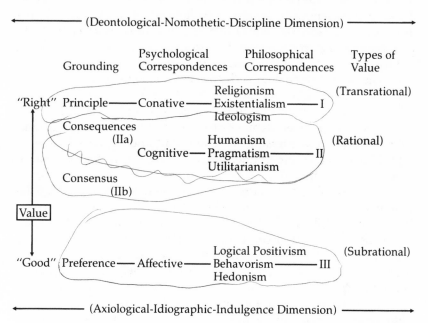

←—————— (Deontological-Nomothetic-Discipline Dimension) ——————→

	Grounding	Psychological Correspondences	Philosophical Correspondences	Types of Value
"Right"	Principle—Conative—	Religionism Existentialism — I Ideologism	(Transrational)
	Consequences (IIa)	Humanism Cognitive— Pragmatism — II Utilitarianism	(Rational)
	Consensus (IIb)		
Value			
"Good"	Preference—Affective—	Logical Positivism Behavorism — III Hedonism	(Subrational)

←—————— (Axiological-Idiographic-Indulgence Dimension) ——————→

The first distinction drawn in the model is to break apart the basic concept of value into its two components of the "right" and the "good". This is the difference between the "desirable" and the "desired"[3] and is technically known as the distinction between the axiological (good) and the deontological (right). The former refers to what is enjoyable, likable, pleasurable; the latter to what is proper, "moral". dutybound, or simply what *ought* to be. Good is known directly as a matter of preference. We do not need to be told what is good (although Madison Avenue continually tries) because we already *know*. We drink when we are thirsty and prefer beer. Or tea. The knowledge of good comes spontaneously from impulse or direct introspection and is a kind of value experience we have in common with other animals. It may be innate, biochemical, genetic, or else learned, programmed, conditioned. It is part of our biological make-up and is essentially hedonistic, summed up in the elemental psychology of seeking pleasure and avoiding pain. It gives rise to no internal value conflict (hence non-human animals do not have "value problems"), but creates the potential for external inter-human value conflict in the general competition for satisfaction from limited resources.

The other dimension of value is the one which really causes the trouble, and it is logically different. We have (although it will be denied by some philosophers) a moral sense, or sense of collective responsibility, a conscience, or perhaps, psychologically speaking, a "superego". At the personal level, this gives rise to a kind of internal conflict—two desirables warring within the bosom of a single self—as we feel on the one side the pull of affect and on the other demands of the situation and what ought to be done. It is the common experience of the discipline of daily life when we forego our self-indulgent desires in favor of other more nomothetic demands. It gets us out of bed in the morning.

But how are these demands to be justified? Upon what grounds do we override our pressing emotive claims and impulses? How can one validate, justify, determine, rank-order given concepts of the desirable in given contexts?

The first column of Figure 2 classifies the several grounds for value judgments and is, as far as I have been able to determine, exhaustive. We can only establish our values in one of these four ways. If we grant that consequences (IIa) and consensus (IIb) can be regarded as subtypes of a single Type II value ground, this then gives us three distinctive types of value. Let us consider them briefly in turn, from the "bottom" up.

Type III values are self-justifying, since they are grounded in individual affect and constitute the individual's preference structure. Why is x good? Because I like it. Why do I like it? I like it because I like it. I cannot go beyond that. Type III values are primitives, facts of nature, justifiable only because the world is what it is and not some other thing.

Moving upwards in the hierarchy, there are three ways in which a value can be adjudged as *right*. First, if it concurs with the will of a majority in a given collectivity, the collectivity of context. This is the ground of consensus and yields Type IIb values. Second, if upon reasonable analysis of the consequences entailed by the pending value judgment, some future resultant state of affairs is held to be desirable, then this is Type IIa value. Type II values enlist the reason, the cognitive faculty, whether it be to count heads (IIb) or to assess contingencies (IIa); the grounds are *social* for they depend upon collectivities and collective justification. The analysis of consequences presupposes a social context and a given scheme of social norms, expectations and standards. If the reasoning is used purely to "figure the odds" on an expedient basis to the end of maximizing individual hedonic satisfaction then this would not be Type IIa but rather Type III value behavior. It should also be noted that Type IIa values beg the question of grounds insofar as they project into the future the state of desirability. The grounds of that projected desirability must be adjudged either on Type

I or Type IIb grounds or even, as the logical positivists would argue, upon the collective preferential grounds of Type III.

Lastly, there are Type I values. The grounding of Type I values is metaphysical. We can concede this without apology. I have called such grounds grounds of principle. The principles take the form of ethical codes, injunctions or commandments, such as the Kantian categorical imperative or the Mosaic "Thou shalt not kill," but whether they derive from a postulated moral insight, an asserted religious revelation, or an aesthetic sense of individual drama, their common feature is that they are unverifiable by the techniques of science and cannot be justified by merely logical argument. The farthest that rational argument can lead is to an ethic of enlightened self-interest. But this is essentially Type IIa in grounding, a sort of game theory solution to the problem of maximizing hedonic (Type III) satisfactions. Type I values have, moreover, a quality of absoluteness which distinguishes them from the more relative Type III values. Principles are also transrational in that, while they need not conflict with rationality, they may equally well do so and may be, in fact from a Type II standpoint, perverse, irrational, absurd as, say, when human sacrifice of the Kamikaze variety is grounded in extreme patriotism or when one finds murder desirable on existential grounds (Camus, Dostoevski). The characteristic of Type I values is that they are based on the will rather than upon the reasoning faculty; their adoption implies some kind of act of faith, belief, commitment.

The second column of Figure 2 shows the psychological correspondences for each of the three types of value. Type III values are rooted in the emotional structure; they are affective, idiosyncratic, idiographic and direct. They are basically a-social and hedonistic. Type II values engage the reasoning faculty; they are preeminently rational, cognitive, collective and social. To the extent that they conflict with and override tendencies to individual indulgence, they are disciplinary and nomothetic. They tend to an ethic of enlightened self-interest or some form of humanistic liberalism, this being as far as logic and the cognitive faculty can go in the determination of an ethic or system of cohesive moral imperatives. Type I values invoke the will. An act of faith or commitment is necessary. This act can only be done on an individual basis, and so, in a sense, Type I values are highly idiographic, although they may be nomothetically endorsed. Let me illustrate.

A ballet company endorses artistic merit, a military organization subscribes to the value of patriotism, a football team is dedicated to winning. In each case, Type I values are set up which must be individually adopted by the sweating dancer, the bleeding soldier, and the bruised player. Dancer, soldier, and player must each, at some point, have made some act of personal commitment to the respective value. If

Commitment — in 4 Component Model

they have not, they may still accept the degraded Type I value at the level of consensus, Type IIb, that is, as a norm or level of expectation peculiar to that collectivity. Needless to say, there is a change in the quality of commitment if this is the case, and administrators would generally prefer to induce the higher level type of engagement in subordinates. More than the member's reason must have been involved where Type I values are operative, and this *more* is not a simple matter of emotive preference. Because of this more, because of the deontological or duty aspect of value, any discussion of the value concept leads easily into questions about the phenomena of loyalty, commitment, guilt, conscience, and responsibility. These concepts are difficult at both the philosophical and the psychological levels of analysis, but they refer generally to those personal experiences of internal states of tension between the types of value portrayed in the two arms of the model.

The figure also shows in the third column some of the main philosophical correspondences. Type III values are those which lend themselves to the reductions of logical positivism and behaviorism. In the extreme case, we can argue that *all* values are mere expressions of emotive preference. To declare "murder is wrong" or "one should not kill" is only to say "Murder, ugh!" or "I do not *like* killing."[4]One may counter that this position simultaneously commits the naturalistic fallacy and unjustifiably elevates logic and science above ethics and values (itself an emotive preference), but the strength of the arguments underlying it are not to be underestimated and, in administrative philosophy, the position is exemplified by Simon. Again, at the sociological level, the so-called playboy and hippie philosophies of self-indulgence are by no means inconsistent with the positivist position.

Type II values, as already indicated, correspond to the philosophical positions of humanism, utilitarianism, and pragmatism. They are buttressed by the social status quo, and the ethos, mores, laws, customs and traditions of a given culture. In general, reason and compromise are venerated, and the subscription to prudence and expediency makes such philosophical orientations particularly attractive to administrators.

Type I values have metaphysical or transrational grounds. In consequence, they are often codified into religious systems. Such systems can, of course, be quite atheistic, as in Communism and in some forms of Buddhism. They can also be deliberately irrational or perhaps antirational, as where the Nazi recruit swears a blood oath in the forest or the French existentialist, convinced that the universe is alien and absurd, yet seeks "authenticity" by "becoming engaged" to a code of values. Once again, to the logical positivist such values are either lit-erally non-sense or else they, like Type II values, are disguised expres-sions of affect—emotive preference at one or two removes. We need not enter the arguments between philosophical schools at this point—our object is only to comprehend the model—but we may note that while the positivists reject the upper dimension altogether, the adherents of Type II values must walk a razor's edge between the chasms of positiv-istic nihilism on the one side and metaphysical absurdity on the other.[5]

Definition and Understanding

The matter of definition has been elided in the above model in favor of showing the internal structure or logic of the value concept itself. Values are synonymous with meaning in the sense that we live within an invisible world of meaning in which the objective referents or contents of experience are distinct from whatever meaning or value we might ascribe to them. Try, for example, the simple experiment of substituting the word "value" for "meaning" whenever the latter occurs in the following quotation.

> Reflect for a moment on the *world of meaning* in which you live—in which all people really live. What is meaning for you? You want food, say, or you wish to get some appointment or to see some-one. All this is meaning—different meanings in the world of meaning. Now is this meaning tangible or visible? I do not see how you can say that meaning can be touched with the organs of sense or seen by the eye or heard or smelt or tasted. For example, money has meaning to everyone. But is the meaning of money touchable or seeable? It is surely not an object of any of the senses. As an object of the senses it can take any form—paper silver, gold, scrip, or just credit—but the meaning *remains* the same quite apart from the visible form. It is necessary to point this out as people often take an object and its meaning as identical....[6]

One might add that it is an only too common administrative error, with profound implications for leadership, to seek value and meaning in some sort of objective way, either by reference to the world of fact (which in truth is meaningless) or, at one remove, in some so-called consensus of opinion.

For our purposes here, values (meanings) can be defined as con-cepts of the desirable with motivating force. This is, of course, tauto-logical if it be assumed that all human action is motivated by desire. It is easier to define than to understand but, for our purposes, we can adopt,

without context or argument, the more elaborate definition first framed
by Kluckhohn:

> A value is a conception, explicit or implicit, distinctive of an indi-
> vidual or characteristic of a group, of the desirable which influ-
> ences the selection from available modes, means, and ends of
> action.[7]

Such values may be characterized in various ways as, say, political,
moral, religious, aesthetic, economic, but as I have sought to explain
them they are phenomenological entities intermediate between motives (which may or may not be accessible to inspection) and attitudes.
Values may be organized into clusters which reflect in attitudinal orientations and general predispositions to act. They are of three types, with
respective psychological and philosophical correspondences. Some
degree of value conflict is the normal human condition. Even more so is
it the administrative condition. Our ultimate goal is to explore the possibilities of an administrative philosophy which will provide techniques and justification for the right resolution of conflicts of value and
interest. Sophistication about the nature of value is a necessary prerequisite to this end.

Postulates

The model of value or value paradigm carries with it some far-
reaching implications. These extend both to the problem of the resolution of value conflicts and to the formulation of value theory or philosophy. For example, the model implies that the value problem is a
universal feature of the human condition and is defined by the tension
which exists between the lower dimension of indulgence and the
upper dimension of denial. Everyone, with the possible exceptions of
saints, supermen, and psychopaths experiences this dialectical tension.
For the saint it disappears because he *wishes* to do what *ought* to be
done; affect and will are unified. And for the Nietzschean Superman
there is again no ambivalence, for what he wishes *is* what is right: he is
jenseits Guete und Boese, beyond Good and Evil. But ordinary people lead
lives of inner conflict; they are exposed to the warring clash of moral
codes without and to the internal stress between the value dimensions
within. The conflict is not simply a matter of the desirable versus the
desired, it is as likely to be between two or more desirables or between
two or more desireds. We have to choose between rights and between
goods, as well as between right and good. Taken together with the continuous interplay of interest which is intrinsic to organizational behavior, this value complexity substantiates Barnard's claim[8] that the

critical contribution of administrative leadership is a capacity for the creative resolution of moral conflicts.

The model also suggests three postulates:

Postulate 1: Hierarchy. Implicit in the model is the idea that Type I values are superior, more authentic, better justified, of more defensible grounding than Type II. Likewise, Type II superior to Type III; and the nomothetic or moral dimension to the idiographic or indulgent dimension. There is a hierarchy of rank.

Postulate 2: Degeneration. Values tend to lower their level of grounding over time. There is a natural tendency for values to lose their authenticity or force. The force of moral insight attenuates.

Postulate 3: Avoidance. There will be a natural tendency to resolve value conflicts at the lowest level of hierarchy possible in a given situation. We seek to avoid moral issues. This applies particularly in administration.

Let me illustrate these postulates by examples from ethics, aesthetics, and administration.

The notion of adultery as a wrong (and conversely of marital fidelity as a positive good) may originally have been instituted by a creative moral thinker or moral leader on bases of moral insight, intuition and conviction. In the course of time and with public acceptance, this institution might degenerate, its original moral force might be weakened, but the value can still be justified on prudential, expedient, pragmatic grounds such as enlightened self-interest; it being argued at the cognitive level, for example, that a society in which adultery is disapproved may be on the whole more functional or beneficial than one in which it is not. Again, the force of this cognitive moral reasoning may weaken and degenerate until fidelity or non-adultery becomes a mere norm or social expectation of the majority. Finally, all moral force may be spent and the value becomes merely a matter of individual preference. One does one's own thing, subject only to the reality constraints provided by the moral vestiges of marital law and societal norms.

From aesthetics let us take the example of, say, Turner's paintings. These may have been conceived by the artist on the basis of deep insight into nature, profound conceptions which he than strove to render in his work. Initially they were not understood or appreciated by critics lacking these insights, but with the passage of time, they were defended at the cognitive or intellectual level by, in this instance, the critic Ruskin. Eventually, larger numbers of aesthetes were persuaded of their value and in time the appreciation of Turner became an aesthetic norm, or social convention. Finally, this level of justification could also pass and it would be argued that the works have value over other works only in accord with individual preference; beauty is entirely subjective and in the end, nihilistically, everything (or nothing) is beautiful. The original vision is no longer transmitted even dimly through the intellect or the lenses of social convention but, if at all, darkly through idle and fleeting preference.

The postulate of avoidance has been called by Broudy the "principle of least principle"[9] and he gives as an example the case where blacks marching against housing discrimination (a moral issue) are arrested on the count of traffic obstruction (a relatively trivial norm). Again, a student guilty of cheating is expelled on the grounds of non-payment of fees and the conflict is avoided at the moral level by being resolved at the normative level.

More generally, we can state that it is an aim of bureaucracy to rationalize and routinize procedures for the resolution of value issues at the level of least organizational cost. The administrative-managerial preference for the avoidance of moral issues or contests of principle can also be explained by the fact that lower-level resolutions may be amenable to compromise and persuasion, whereas higher-level conflicts may be irreconcilable—not just moral but mortal.

Metavalues

Quite apart from competition among themselves and independent of the idiographic value structures of their administrators and members, organizations (including schools and colleges) can be morally negative. It may, perhaps, be more accurate to describe organizations as morally primitive value environments. I mean to say that, without committing the biological fallacy, organizations tend to be governed by value imperatives which would correspond, in the individual, to the lower levels of self-interest. These imperatives pervade the organization but are most potent and close to the surface of consciousness in the administrative-managerial subsystem. They may be described as *metavalues.*

A metavalue is a concept of the desirable so vested and entrenched that it seems to be beyond dispute or contention. It usually enters as an unspoken or unexamined assumption into the ordinary value calculus of individual or collective life. Examples of metavalues would be wealth or life itself. In a democratic society, democracy is a metavalue; amongst academics, education, rationality and consistency are common metavalues. It is not so much that metavalues are absolute or quasi-absolute as that they go, for the most part, unquestioned, *beyond* value, and so intrude unconsciously to affect value behavior. Let us now consider the principal organizational metavalues.

Maintenance

It has been said that the first law of nature is self-preservation. Extrapolating to the collectivity, the first law of organization is survival. The organization must maintain itself. In new and emerging organizations this metavalue is patently obvious, but it can recede from the conscious level as the association, organization or institution becomes established and secure. Once in existence, an organization does not question its need-to-be. The attendant values of organizational loyalty are rapidly proliferated and form the basis of the value indoctrination of new members. Though threats to the collective interests of organization members may close their ranks and raise the level of consciousness of the maintenance value, it does not follow that the actual best means to survival will be selected. Organizations may sometimes appear to the outside observer to be suicidal—the trade union, for example, which puts its employers and itself out of business—but this only serves to prove that factual rationality is distinct from valuational trans- or sub-rationality.

For the administrator, it goes without saying (it is beyond value question) that the first obligation is to maintain the organization. Without the organization, there is nothing to administer. This does not deny the occasional administrative function of eliminating dysfunctional subsystems. Such elimination would be in the interests of the whole organization, the largest unit of employment of the administrator. Katz and Kahn express it as follows: "Since any organization must survive in order to carry out its basic functions, survival becomes a salient goal for ogranizational decision makers. [Dynamic forces generated by maintenance structures] have as their implicit, and sometimes explicit, goal the survival of present organizational forms. For many administrators and officials, concern with the preservation of the bureaucracy assumes primary significance. Indeed, the term bureaucracy is often used, not in the Weberian sense, but in the sense of an officialdom absorbed only in the preservation of its structure and in the ease of its own operation."[10]

The maintenance metavalue is nomothetic. It is a fundamental part of the administrator's value bias. To rise above this bias it would be necessary first to ask the unaskable question, Should my organization exist?

Growth

The second metavalue is growth. Organizations seek to expand; their dynamic finds form in extension. Merely to survive and maintain the status quo is not enough. Resources are always limited and the normal condition is competition for their control. This applies to corporate as well as to individual bodies and to public corporations as well as to private. It also applies intraorganizationally, and the study of bureaucracy is replete with instances of dysfunction traceable to this impulse and metavalue. Growth can also be conceived as protective insofar as it augments power and thus protects against threats to survival. In this way it is corollary to the first metavalue.

But organizations are not biological entities. They are coherences of interest and it is this coherence, or economy of incentives as Barnard calls it, which must grow if the metavalue is to be actualized. Barnard accepts the innate propensity for expansion and analyses the metavalue in this way:

> The maintenance of incentives, particularly those relating to prestige, pride of association, and community satisfaction, calls for growth, enlargement, extension. It is, I think, the basic and, in a sense, the legitimate reason for bureaucratic aggrandizement in corporate, governmental, labor, university, and church organizations everywhere observed. To grow seems to offer opportunity for the realization of all kinds of active incentives—as may be observed by the repeated emphasis in all organizations upon size as an index of the existence of desirable incentives, or the alternative rationalization of other incentives when size is small or growth often so upsets the economy of incentives, through its reactions upon the effectiveness and efficiency of organization, that it is no longer possible to make them adequate.[11]

The caution against overexpansion is to be noted. The status of growth as a metavalue is less secure than that of maintenance. From time to time it is consciously acknowledged that bigness does not of itself provide the necessary and sufficient conditions for goodness; and it is well known that growth can be cancerous and dysfunctional. On the other hand, the logic of survival is to place as many bulwarks as possible between target and threat. Many subordinates rather than few can mean more protective cover, sacrificial cover if need be. And organizational expansion, even in non-threatening supportive environments, serves to preclude the birth or growth of potential competitors. Growth can mean power (itself an administrative metavalue) and to gain power is a natural administrative reflex. Therefore, a bias toward growth is corollary to that toward maintenance. To challenge this metavalue is to challenge the second law of organization and the natural tendency of systems.

Effectiveness and Efficiency

An organization is effective if it can achieve its purposes, and conversely. It follows that there is an imperative to be effective and that effectiveness is an organizational metavalue. How can this be contested? To point to the factual evidence of many existing ineffective organizations does not refute the metavalue; such evidence merely suggests that there is some measure (intuitive or objective) of organizational success and that on this standard (or metavalue) organizations can be perceived to be deficient. What in personal language is called success, though here with overtones of fame, reputation and power, is in organizational terms called effectiveness. Effectiveness is the accomplishment of desired ends. As a metavalue it is tautologous, for it means the desirability of accomplishing desired ends, and because of this tautology it goes unexamined. The only way in which it can be challenged, short of re-examining the ends themselves, is by a consideration of what sociologists call latent functions. These are the unforeseen, unintended or unpredictable side effects which are consequences of any means-end chain of action initiated by the pursuit of goals. Sometimes these latent functions may be foreseen, intended, and tacitly recognized. For example, a conference of administrators may have as its manifest function the reading and discussion of presented papers, but this function may be valuationally outweighed by the concomitant social intercourse and interaction (especially where expense accounts can be billed for the occasion). In such a case, the *ad hoc* organization (the conference and its arrangements) is effective if the latent functions are fulfilled and due propriety observed with respect to the manifest functions. The metavalue of effectiveness appears to be the one metavalue which is incontestable—because of tautology—but it can on scrutiny give rise to questions about the sought and unsought consequences of the ends of action.

Efficiency is a term which has caused some confusion in the classical literature due to its divergent usage by Barnard. Barnard related efficiency to the satisfaction of individual motives. This is consistent with his view of organizations as incentive collectivities. Organizations were for him "efficient" insofar as they succeeded in eliciting sufficient individual co-operation. The efficiency of a co-operative system would be its capacity to maintain itself by the individual satisfactions it affords.

Simon's usage is more conventional. Efficiency is essentially the ratio of input to output and can be conceived in engineering terms. A transformer is 80% efficient if that is the ratio of wattage delivered to wattage at the input terminals. Monetary measures of efficiency form the bases of economic accountancy. The primary fact of economic life is scarcity of resources, and consciousness of this underlies all administrative decisions and establishes a criterion of choice wherein one seeks the largest result or pay-off for any given application of resources. I shall take the term in this ordinary sense, and consider it a metavalue, because on the face of it no administrator will consciously choose, *ceteris paribus,* the less efficient of two alternatives. But let us look at this great basic assumption of administration more closely.

The efficiency metavalue implies that (a) given alternative means with the same cost attaching to each means, one will seek the maximum return, that is, maximization of ends; (b) given alternative goals with the same end value one will choose ends so as to minimize the cost of means. In both (a) and (b) there are two possible sources of fallacy, the one having to do with the meaning and specification of costs and the other with the meaning and specification of goals or ends. In all of this, there are major conceptual obstacles which include the incommensurability of quantification and quality, the imponderability of the value and intentional factors in decision making, and the problem of ascertaining all cost and benefit functions. Efficiency as a metavalue is applied forward, to the future; but as a value it is measured backwards, in respect of the past. Perhaps this explains why, from the standpoint of retrospective wisdom, so much inefficiency is to be observed in organizations. But it remains a metavalue, and to challenge it is to open up all the issues of administrative philosophy. Administrators cannot choose to value inefficiency but can probe, if they wish, the devious and sometimes intractable implications of the efficiency metavalue itself.

Other candidates may be proposed for the status of metavalue, for example, rationality and power. However, upon reflection it will be seen that these can generally be subsumed under the four metavalues already described. Thus, rationality and power are implicit with the desirability concepts of efficiency and effectiveness. But because these values are endemic to all forms of organization and because they pass unquestioned and unexamined, a problem is posed for the moral leader by the value character of the very organization he would purport to lead.

Organizations as Moral Primitives

I would reiterate that the four metavalues described above refer to organizations rather than to individuals. They are universal organizational values. Taken together, they constitute the desire or volition bases for collective systems, and, when conceived as organizational laws, they form quasi-moral imperatives or commandments for the administrator: or perhaps one single injunction, "Thou shalt not destroy thine organization." There is then a progression by way of the positive corollary to, "Seek the organization's interest always!" and by easy stages of increasing identification with *us* (organization members) and disidentification with *them* (non-organization members) to "What's good for General Motors is good for the country" and, finally, "My country, right or wrong." Perhaps, but even without any extrapolation, the conventional wisdom is that the administrator must maintain the organization, must seek its growth wherever opportunity for growth is discerned, must seek the accomplishment of the organization's goals, and throughout must seek these ends as efficiently as possible. This primitive value structure or base has imperative force for the leader prior to and without regard for personal value orientation. And this force will apply whether he or she is actively conscious of it or not. It is in this way that we can consider organizations to be morally "primitive", the collectivity is neither person nor biological entity, but its structure of interest and its constitution as a corporate entity establish *ipso facto* a value pattern with governing effect on its administrators, and this pattern, measured against humane individual standards, can be called elemental, primitive or unsophisticated.

This does not mean that organizations are of necessity corrupting or degrading to the moral or value life of their members, but that they can work this subtly negative influence if their primitive imperatives are allowed to impose themselves, achieve dominance, or go unexamined. An efficient organization effectively maintaining itself, expanding its influence, achieving its goals, can be wondrous to behold and a source of beneficence to those inside and outside it. It can also be a Juggernaut, a moral anathema, an engine of corruption. The prophylactic is fairly simple to prescribe. It is to be found in the periodic re-examination of the metavalues. This will raise for reflection the following questions.

1. Is the organization unjustified in its basic purpose?
2. Is the organization unjustified in its complex of ancillary purposes?
3. Should the organization grow? consolidate? reduce? Is the growth pattern valid and defensible?
4. What are the latent functions of the organizational effort and are they valid or defensible?
5. What, so far as resonable analysis can reveal, is the shape of the non-quantitative cost benefit account? Is the quality of organizational life adequate under its constraints?

6. What consistency exists between the answers to these value
    questions and (a) Type II morality, (b) the Type I commitments
    of the administrator?

It is *not* suggested (unless this be directly brought out by the metavalue
analysis itself) that a full re-examination of organizational policy and
philosophy be undertaken. That is a matter of administrative philosophy at large; the point of metavalue scrutiny is simply to reduce their
primitive unconscious influence and reenter them into the value calculus of administration at a more conscious and sophisticated level.

To this point I have been talking of organizations as moral primitives. It is logically possible, though psychologically unlikely, that
there are individual administrators who are similarly primitive. The
leader, too, has his or her individual metavalue counterparts of *personal*
maintenance, growth, efficiency and effectiveness. To these we can
probably add, as corollaries, the instrumental metavalue of power and
the end metavalue of success. The private metavalue system is as
deserving of periodic re-examination as is the organizational, but it is
distinct and can be considered as a separate subset of administrative
philosophy.

Metavalues are by definition *good*. The question is always whether
they are *right*. To even ask that question implies a degree of sophistication, consciousness and moral complexity which at least augurs to
obviate or mitigate any charge of primitiveness.

Having now considered at some length the general theory of
value and having established a general paradigm, we can proceed to
examine their workings in the practice or, more correctly, *praxis* of
administration and leadership.

6

Value Praxis

How is theory related to practice? The question is a difficult one whether it refers to organizational theory, management theory, political theory, or value theory. In the whirl of everyday practice, the direct presence of theory may not be felt. It may indeed be considered irrelevant or, worse, counter-functional. But, despite all denials, it is there. Implicit or tacit theory always underlies the behavior and actions of the leader. The function of this book is simply to raise the level of consciousness about what is hidden, and to bring it into the light. In other words, to ground action on better theory, on the best theory available. The conscious practice of administration, as opposed to the merely mechanical, the laissez-faire, or the unsophisticated is what is properly called *praxis*. When that word is used with respect to value theory it suggests some concept of *right* value. And here one is reminded of the Confucian doctrine of Rectification of Names. In essence this states that if a name such as *school* has come to be applied to an organization which is *not* a school in the original sense, but rather some sort of arrangement for childholding, job preparation, or social conditioning, then one of three things should take place. Either the school should cease to call itself a school and instead call itself what it now is, say, a care centre or holding facility or social programming unit, or the shift in language should be recognized so that all now understand what the name properly signifies and denotes, or it should change to fit the original definition.

Likewise, if a leader is defined by the attributes of being a gentleman and a man of honor, and if our leaders in fact are liars, rogues and Philistines, then we should cease to call them leaders and instead call them what they are, say, manipulators. Or we should require them to cease being manipulators. Or we should embrace the linguistic shift so that henceforth leader *means* manipulator.

Praxis

What is always implicit should now be explicitly clear. The field of executive action and the administrative endeavor which embraces it make philosophical demands. It is the highest function of the executive to develop a deep understanding of self and of his colleagues, a knowledge of human nature which includes motivation, but reaches beyond it into the domain of value possibilities. After all, the very stuff of the administrative fabric, the warp and woof of organizational life, is protoplasmic—human nature in all its rich diversity, complexity and frequent simplicity. Administrators are voyeurs extraordinary.

Of course, different kinds of people will come to the role of administrator, with different characters and characteristics; with different patterns of values. And their roles will be embedded in different types of organizational context, again with different patterns of values. But whatever the variations of context and role, the philosophical theme will persist and certain philosophical skills will be desirable and appropriate, even for rudimentary survival. At its lowest level, organizational life is a sort of daily combat. Even here, however, the deadliest weapons in the administrative armory are philosophical: the skills of logical and critical analysis, conceptual synthesis, value analysis and commitment, the power of expression in language and communication, rhetoric and, most fundamentally, the depth of understanding of human nature. So in the end, philosophy becomes intrinsically practical. The cartography it provides becomes the administrator's most vital navigational aid. But skill in the use of this armamentarium does not come automatically. It is far more likely (with one proviso) to be acquired through experience and the natural acquisition of seniority. For this reason there may well be wisdom, and a sort of natural justice in the practice—once universal but now most obvious in Japan—of promotion on the sole basis of seniority. The proviso, of course, is that experience be consciously reflective and not the mere passage of time.

It is here that Aristotle has taught us a valuable lesson; a lesson which, strangely, seems to have been forgotten in the West but one which urgently needs to be relearned. It is that man has three distinctive ways of knowing; three approaches to the world, three modes of action. They are *theoria, techné* and *praxis. Theoria,* or theory, represents our knowing function in its purest form as it seeks to abstract, generalize, induce and deduce from a world of sense data that is given and that needs to be explained. It is this state of mind which has dominated in the search for first principles. In its higher reaches, it offers the prospect of *sophia,* that transcendent wisdom of which *philosophy* is supposed to be the lover. Nevertheless, this crowning glory which has done so much, which has given us science and explored the limits of cosmic and microcosmic space, which has unravelled so much of our chemical nature, has yet failed to provide us with a conclusive theory of action or of organization and administration.

What theory has endowed us with most lavishly is *techné*, the mode of knowing which yields productive arrangements of matter and material, indeed, all the arts, crafts and products of man. From this root stem technics, technique, technology, applied science, applied theory. From this cognitive mode comes so much of the structure and quality of modern life: from moonshots to multimedia, from periodontics to pantyhose. Technology liberates as it constrains, imprisons as it frees, seems to possess the peculiar capability of delimiting our horizons at the same time as it expands them, promises the stars then locks us in our bureaucratic cells. In Aristotle's thought *techné* gave rise to *poiesis*, which was a way of treating the reality of the sense world so that artifacts, objects and constructs could be produced. Its exponent was *homo faber*, the productive or creative man: man as artist and artisan and, nowadays, man as applied scientist, technologist, manager, auditor, accountant and clerk.

These distinctions are commonplace and well understood. In fact, they have become oversubscribed with the dichotomy between theory and practice so well entrenched in modern society that it has led to some dangerous divisions in professional life between theorist and practitioner, researcher and developer, academic cloister and field experience, planner and public and, of course, in our terms, between administrator and manager. Such divisions can lead to worse than mere failure of communication, but they stem from a failure of conception. What is missing here is Aristotle's third term, *praxis*.

No direct equivalent exists in the English language for this term but it deserves a better fate than to have been appropriated solely by the Marxists, where it is understood as action with political reflection (that is, with the right ideological consciousness). Aristotle intended the term to mean ethical action in a political context or, simply, purposeful human conduct which would be an amalgam of theory (rationality, science) and values (morals, emotions, ethics). Praxis was thus a complex and subtle, but nonetheless essential, concept. It suggests a duality in action, two moments of consciousness or reflection on the one hand, and behavior and commitment on the other. The contemporary contrast between behavior and action comes close to this distinction but is cruder and more dualistic. Behavior is discernible movement, while action is movement with identified intent. Strict behaviorists might see no need for any present or potential voluntarism in this distinction, but the concept of praxis would insist upon some freedom of choice at the phenomenological level. Praxis would then imply conscious reflective intentional action. Applied to administration, it would mean the combination of management science with ethics and value theory. Praxis is thus a concept uniquely applicable to administration: it could be regarded as the quintessence of administration. But it is a concept which would make intellectual and spiritual demands and perhaps this is why it has become lost to usage. Its principal demands would be within the domains of consciousness and values, and about these topics much more has yet to be said. In the end, however, praxis is what must be explicated because it is the true link between theory and practice, theoria and techné. It is, as is administration, philosophy-in-action.

But what kinds of philosophy? What are the constraints and restrictions peculiar to administration, and to educational leadership? But already another pre-emptive question may have occurred to the reader. Why can we not rest our case and move at once to enunciations of moral philosophy which would bear directly on the field of administration?

Because, I think, of the tendency to simultaneously concede and beg the value question. Having agreed to being beset by value problems, it is not uncommon for executives to exemplify in practice the postulate of avoidance or to retreat into managerialism. This may be excusable; it often is, but what is of deeper concern is the often-encountered reluctance or inability of administrators to provide details of any philosophical commitment (or understanding). An abhorrence is sometimes apparent for any seemingly absolute value proposition or, at least, one in contravention of the cultural absolute that "all values are relative." A retreat to positivism is another way in which the value problem can be begged. A hesitancy about coming to grips with the value question in administration is quite understandable, if not quite forgivable. The complexity alone is a disincentive; the contemplative aspect is a deterrent to the man of action. But the problem must be faced, and explored.

Positivism Revisited

It can be argued that all human behavior is value laden simply by virtue of the fact that, random activity excluded, it is motivated. Administration can therefore claim no particular distinction. The rebuttal to this argument lies in the special collective characteristic of administration. Values in administration refer not simply to the individual person of the administrator, nor even to his or her extended ego in the form of family, clan or interest clique, but to the nomothetic collectivity of the organization. These values are ostensibly of Type II. Nevertheless, it would be quite unrealistic to suppose that the administrator is a mere value functionary of the organization, as Simon at times seems to maintain, nor must we ever lose sight of the idiographic interest complex represented by the administrator, whose own commitment to Type I and Type III values could be crucial.

The problem is difficult. Fields of value interlace and overlap. The temptation to avoid the question altogether is powerful. One technique of avoidance is the retreat to managerialism: separate ends from means and apportion the latter to management, whereby the only value test need then be the criterion of goal accomplishment. Simon, as mentioned, sometimes beats this retreat, but in his philosophical posture he goes further and explicitly espouses the doctrine of logical positivism.[1] He attempts to separate means from ends and facts from values so as to make the former of these pairs the special province of a practical administrative science.[2]

> It is sometimes thought that, since the words 'good' and 'bad' often occur in sentences written by students of administration, the science of administration contains an essential ethical element. If this were true, a science of administration would be impossible, for it is impossible to choose, on an empirical basis, between ethical alternatives. Fortunately, *it is not true.* The terms 'good' and 'bad' when they occur in a study of administration are *seldom* employed in a purely ethical sense. Procedures are termed 'good' when they are conducive to the attainment of *specified objectives*, 'bad' when they are not conducive to such attainment. That they are, or are not, so conducive is purely a matter of *fact*, and it is this factual element which makes up the real substance of an administrative science. To illustrate: In the realm of economics, the proposition 'alternative A is good' may be translated into two propositions, one of them ethical, the other factual.
>
> "Alternative A will lead to maximum profit."
>
> "To maximize profit is good."
>
> The first of these two sentences has no ethical content, and is a sentence of the practical science of business. The second sentence is an ethical imperative, and has no place in any science. (my italics)[3]

Of course we cannot agree, either in fact or in philosophy. The terms "good" and "bad" are, as the value paradigm reveals, often inextricably confused with "right" and "wrong". It is not correct to say that they are seldom used in a purely ethical sense in administrative studies nor, to put it the other way round, that when commonly used they are void of ethical content. The ubiquity of value terminology in administrative literature only goes to show the difficulty of attaining to any administrative *science*. Simon is indirectly asserting that the end justifies the means and, while his position might conceivably have reference to some hypothetical managerial technology, it does not sensibly apply to the activity of administration, least of all to educational leadership. The terms "good" and "bad" may indeed at times be specified by some "objective", and this may reduce the element of value judgment to "near-fact", but reduction is not elimination, and even here the value terms would be materially affected by the larger value culture of the organization. It would depend, for example, on sub-cultural notions about the desirability of efficiency, workmanship, excellence, responsibility and how process-means were related to product-ends. The situation is value-infused, subtle, and subject to continuous modulation. Standards, for example, change over time and place and person. On the other hand, we must agree with Simon that ethical imperatives are non-scientific, but this is only to reiterate what we have been saying all along, that administration is philosophical.

Simon's treatment of the value issue could also appear suspiciously like Type IIa pragmatism—values are assessed in terms of consequences as related to specified objectives—but this only begs the question as to how, in turn, the specified objectives are to be determined and value-judged and this, in the logical positivist mode, returns us to what is essentially Type III positivism. The values are there because they're there and any one set is as ethically valid as any other.

If, then, the philosophical position of logical positivism is adopted, ethical statements tend to vanish by way of the reduction of value judgments to emotive preference. The administrator can deny ethical imperatives by talking only of preferences. The pursuit of the leader's own interest to the exclusion of that of others would be (subject to game rules or organizational constraints) as valid as any other position. This nihilistic view lends a pseudo-scientific atmosphere to the discussion of values in administration, and is one of the way in which serious value debate can be avoided. But there are other kinds of praxis.

Supervision

Administration is a perpetual becoming, a journey in which the destination is never reached. The end of a war is the beginning of a peace; one problem situation dissolves into another. In a sense, for the leader the future is always more real then the present. It is the impending which presses on the mind.

To an extent, this is so even at the level of Simon's divorce between factual means and valuational ends, because organizations always represent states of inadequacy. The inadequacy is the gap between the way things are—the factual state of affairs at a given instant
—and the way things ought to be at some future instant, that of the
consummation of the specified objective. Since the present is always
distinct from the future, and can at most be only a kind of straining
towards some future condition, a state of inadequacy is defined by the
mere act of establishing a future goal or target; it is a price which must
be paid by any purposive entity: the price of intention.

But the ought-to-be, the desirable future state, affects the present
in another and more immediate practical way, through the imperative
to check that the best means are being employed in the best way at any
given instant, so as to achieve the best progression of means to ends
and the best conversion of present into future. I have used the term
"best" four times in the last sentence and the terms "ought", "desirable", and "imperative" once. The value language is inescapable, and
points in this instance to the omnipresence of the metavalues: efficiency and effectiveness, growth and productivity which guide administrative judgments at the nomothetic (Type II) level.

Leaders have a continuous onus or duty or responsibility to monitor their organizations in this way, to seek best means for given ends
and best conduct for given means, even without entering into the
determination of the ends themselves. This is traditionally regarded as
the supervisory function, but it too has ethical imperative elements.

In supervisory or monitoring behavior, the administrator will,
consciously or unconsciously, engage his or her own interests and pattern of motivation. This is one part of the idiographic aspect. Another is
the leader's world view and concept of human nature as these apply to
organizational life. This idiographic structure is simultaneously com-
promised by the nomothetic commitment to the collective values of
the organization. There are, moreover, extra-organizational values
which can serve either as constraints or temptations. (Pollution, crime,
confusion, war could be good for the organization. Overpopulation can
aid school enrollment, and sickness is a requirement for the practice of
medicine). The degree of awareness with which an administrator is
able to enter all of these elements into the decisional calculus and into
the monitoring function is a measure of moral sophistication, of capacity for Barnard's moral complexity.

Still, this is not all. Each organization member is a value actor,
though each need not have the formal allegiance to the nomothetic
realm which is imposed upon the leader. But if the members are not
monitoring, they are being monitored, and it is here that the administrator's knowledge of the informal organization and perception of shifts

in values within the complex of subsystems is called upon. How is this value information to be gathered? If Mintzberg is correct, the administrator will rely upon a private intelligence network and the flow of gossip.[4] This in turn raises the political question of who is controlling the flow of information. Obviously there is at least some scope for power play, intrigue and subversion.

Monitoring not only engages the administrator's philosophy in performance of the nomothetic role, it also raises the problem of organizational speciality. One has an onus to keep oneself informed (in a general way) of advances in technology which bear upon the organization's life, both with respect to ends and to means. Technological advances lead to changes in means, and this can have value implications. Failure to adopt them, their rapid adoption, or their too rapid adoption may affect the organization in its competition for resources, and determine its growth or survival prospects. A change such as automation may have radical effects on organization membership. Quite apart, then, from idiographic value orientation, the administrator must be engaged in a continuous nomothetic value monitoring which is difficult, subtle, protean, and taxing.

Human Nature

Mr. Matsushita, the eminent Japanese industrialist and founder of the Matsushita School of Government and Management, an elite educational establishment devoted to preparing leaders for the twenty-first century, was greatly concerned with the problem of human nature.[5] To reflect upon the truth about human nature was for him a matter of vital importance for leadership and a concern with this topic is central to the curriculum at the Matsushita School. In ordinary praxis, however, the operative concepts of human nature may be greatly oversimplified, often to stereotypical proportions. In general, these may be classified as the traditional, the human relations, or the human resources models of management.[6]

The basic assumption in the traditional model is that work is inherently distasteful for most people, and yet more distasteful is responsibility. Work must therefore be extrinsically motivated, chiefly through the means of pay and security measures. Herzberg's and Maslow's lower-level needs dominate. It follows that monitoring must be rigorous. Teachers and students should not be left unsupervised nor should subordinates be left to their own devices. Caution should prevail over trust. In general, people are above all self-seeking, they will take advantage if they can, and they are notoriously incompetent. They adulate power and despise weakness. Therefore work should be designed to stress simplification of tasks, routinization of decisions and clear lines of authority and command. The time clock and the punch card are essential. Hierarchy is the natural order. Fear is the prime mover.

The logic extends to principals and other line administrators as well as staff. It is a safe assumption that they too are selfish and greedy, but in contrast to staff they may not be lazy, and instead may be power-hungry and ambitious. These features can be capitalized upon, as for example by designing hierarchial ladders for the upwardly mobile underlings to climb.

In general, the meta-assumption behind the postulated assumptions of the traditional model seems to be the notion that it is safest in collective enterprise to assume the worst of the collective constituents. In that way one can only be happily surprised. The same principle underlies conservative accounting practice, conservative economics and, generally, wherever people talk of "keeping each other honest."

The human relations model rejects simple self-centeredness and stresses instead the social aspect of human nature. People seek social gratifications, acceptance and recognition by their peers, group satisfactions, some sense of belongingness. We move into the upper reaches of Maslow's and Herzberg's schemes. Type III values yield to Type II. Status is important. Men, as Napoleon said, are led by baubles. They can be manipulated. Money is only one mark of status, one of the motivators. Subordinates like to be considered and should be treated considerately, informed of organizational affairs, catered to in their informal groupings. The reach of the organization should extend into the extra-organizational life of its members. Contented cows yield more milk. It is better to persuade than to command. The techniques of group dynamics and the manipulative findings of social psychology afford ways in which the harsher truths of Theory X and the traditional model can be glossed over. Administration must be concerned about morale, organizational climate, *esprit de corps*. Political skill is the prime mover. The modal value is Type IIb.

All these principles apply with even extended force to administrative personnel. The shape of Whyte's "Organization Man" begins to appear: conformist, other-directed, a creature of his organization. The human relations leader is genial, smooth, suave, highly manipulative, spiritually empty, unauthentic to the core. Machiavelli knew this person well and it is to be carefully noted that Machiavelli would have endorsed *both* the traditional model and the human relations model.

The human resources model rejects manipulation, denies the distastefulness of work, and bases its presuppositions on Maslow's highest levels of needs. Democratic biases are also evident. People like to work if it is fulfilling, especially if they have had some say in the determination of work and in shaping the organization's objectives.

They can be creative and can enjoy responsibility. Each individual represents a wealth of resources which can be tapped by right administration. The field of organizational life can be structured so as to provide occasions for self-fulfillment. Even discovery of purpose and life-meaning can come from work. Democracy is the natural order. Love is the prime mover. Authenticity and Type I values are to triumph over and synthesize those of Type II and III.

Again the stereotypic human resources view of people can be applied to executives as well as to subordinates. Indeed with even more force, because it is likely in the hierarchical nature of things that the opportunities for the creative exercise of inner resources, for authentic responsibility and moral complexity, will be greatest of all in the administrative-managerial ranks. However, that administrator X wishes the human resources model to be applied by superiors does not necessarily entail that the administrator will apply it to subordinates in turn.

These three praxis orientations are not necessarily mutually exclusive. They are model stereotypes which are held, purely or in combination, by administrators, and which carry implications for administrative style and practice. It would follow that, within the limits of technological and economic constraint, work can and should be designed so as to best exemplify the particular model adopted. I do not wish to contest, at this point, either the veracity of these models or the empirical support for their adoption in the field. It will suffice at present to concede that the administrator's view of human nature becomes an effective part of organizational life, one of the ways in which values intrude into administrative practice and a facet of administrative philosophy.

Nomothetic Bias

It is true that each administrator has a personal idiographic scheme of values and a unique value biography. This has to be reconciled with the special and obligatory nomothetic commitment to the organizational values. This reconciliation is facilitated in a number of ways, the most significant of which, perhaps, stems from the fact that administrators control the organizational reward system. They are, thus, on the face of it more identified with the organizational interest; organizational success is more proportionately meaningful to them than to other classes of members. What is good for the organization is good for them, although, as is often overlooked, what is bad for the organization is often *less* bad for them, especially if they have *de facto* or *de jure* tenure. (That the captain is the last to leave the sinking ship may mean in the real world of administration that he is the *only* survivor.)

Again, because of greater relative rewards, and usually greater status, administrators are prepared to work harder and longer than other organization members. The empirical evidence for this is strong[7] and supports the literary stereotype of the tireless executive. All of this dynamism and the visible attachment to role tends to identify the administrator with nomothetic values.

It is not uncommon to ascribe to successful administrators at least a sympathy for the variously called Puritan, Prussian, Protestant or Work ethics. This general value orientation, made much of by Weber in *The Protestant Ethic and the Spirit of Capitalism*,[8] is typified by self-denial, hard work, deferred gratifications, future-time orientation and a general belief that industry, discipline, authority and productivity are good. It would be a distortion to assert that administrators as a class subscribe to this ethic on a Type I basis, but workaholism is hardly a disqualification for the leadership role and it is legitimate to draw attention to a natural affinity for this ethic, so much so that it might exist as an administrative value bias. Work must tend to rank highly as a value for executive personnel because it provides self-fulfilling opportunities and because of its structured linkage to the hierarchical reward system.

Societal Bias

Extra-organizational cultural values impinge in many ways upon the educational organization. Where leadership is exercised at the board or policy-making level it could perhaps be argued that because of the tenuous or amateur nature of organizational membership at this level, compared to the permanent or tenured levels of full-time salaried personnel, leadership may be more sensitive to extra-organizational interests. On the other hand, it is also certain that the professional administrator cannot afford to be unaware of the context of social motivation. There has been, for example, a contemporary shift to an emergent cultural value orientation which is more permissive and consummatory in character than the traditional pattern. There are also various causes or movements—towards greater power-sharing on behalf of minorities, women, the environment and so forth—which, in the interests of the organization, the administrator will be monitoring, along with any Type IIb shifts of consensus. Where conflict exists between societal and organizational values, the possibility will also exist for a failure of authenticity, and the conditions for an administrative ethical decision will be established.

In general, we can conceive of a progression of interest from (1) the administrator's idiographic value orientation to (2) nomothetic value orientation to (3) the societal value orientation and its consensus in the conventional morality. At each juncture in this progression, opportunities for value conflict will be maximized and so, concomitantly, will opportunities for failure of authenticity. By failure of authenticity we mean not so much a fault in valuation, such as incorrect reasoning, but the deliberate concealment of the operative value (as where self-interest is pursued but group interest professed). It would be unreasonable to expect, in anything short of totalitarian fantasy, a unification of value along the line of progression from individual to community. The natural condition is one of continuous conflict continuously modulated. A pluralistic society will multiply and intensify the breaks in the value progression; it will also intensify the demand for administrative moral complexity. Obviously an instrument or technique for resolving value issues would be desirable.

The model expounded in the previous chapter can be used as such a tool, but its use will always be relative to the social context of its employment, and it implies that the value actor who is disposed to resolve issues at the Type II level—the typical administrative mode—may be at a situational disadvantage in a pluralistic society relative to those whose value positions are extreme. The religious, the ideologically committed, as well as those in passionate pursuit of self-interest, have, as it were, a methodology of decision at their disposal which permits them to see quickly and easily where value conflict can be resolved, where their interests lie, and which concept of the desirable should be allowed to prevail. By contrast, the rational administrator seeking consensus, compromise and consideration of consequences may be less able to perceive any easy or right answer. The issue is "sicklied o'er with the pale cast of thought" and "the native hue of resolution" is lost. The dogmatic, the committed, the aggressive, the self-seekers can often carry the day. And this potential "weakness of the centre" will be all the more likely in a societal context of cultural pluralism and moral relativism.

Summary

Let us recapitulate briefly. Values in praxis are organized about foci of interest. Interest and value are omnipresent in any administrative action. The problems they present cannot be easily disposed of either by arbitrary adoption of a positivistic position *à la* Simon or by abandonment to psychologism or moral relativism. Although the temptation is great to give up in the face of moral complexity, we can distinguish natural trends of bias as indicated, for example, by the metavalues and the nomothetic dimesnion and we can discern the basic positions adopted by administrators with respect to human nature. We are also able to discern the basic praxis problem of organizational malevolence.

Organizational Malevolence

It can be argued that formal organizations and bureaucracy are in certain critical aspects antagonistic to ordinary morality, that is, to Type II conventions and the Type I ethics summed up in the Kantian imperatives. This antagonism comes about because of the organizational value of rationality and the nomothetic principle of depersonalization. School systems, some schools, and most colleges and universities are today complex bureaucratic organizations. In a complex bureaucracy, individuals are not whole persons but role incumbents, partial sets of skills which are of utility to the organizational whole. They are parts, replaceable and substitutable parts at that, In the organization, rationally construed, no one is indispensable. Morality, in glaring contrast, is a function of total personality and this latter exceeds and overflows any role. (Especially, one might think, should this be the case in education.)

In any event, it does not matter what such personalities feel or think, for the organizational language game determines the values appropriate for the social or collective decisions which are made in its name. Organizational goals combined with rational procedures for their attainment (glossed and glazed where necessary by the refinements of the human relations movement) make organizational life analogous to chess. Within the game there are no right or wrong moves, only those of more or less efficacy given the set system of rules, which cannot in itself be challenged. The ordinary organization member can become a logical factotum, alienated or manipulated. Even that extraordinary member, the administrator, is not an author of acts but an agent, one who does things in the name of others.

There is a special way in which the educational leader can be irresponsible. This would be by philosophical and psychological detachment—by the belief that the organization or system is bigger than any individual and possesses a destiny and logic of its own. The leader then commits the biological fallacy and worse; the organization is not only reified, but deified. And the agent is not personally or morally responsible for the acts which are under the authority or authorship of the collectivity. Bureaucrats and civil servants, administrators of industry and education, no less than Adolf Eichmann, must faithfully execute

policies of which they personally disapprove. Thus, outwardly benevolent organizations can become latent collective forces for evil. Or, less
dramatically, schools can go wrong. Perhaps very wrong.

The Leader as Agent

We are not concerned here with the legal aspects of agency, but
rather with the socio-psychological ramifications of collective or social
decision making where the administrator's decision is imputed to the
organization. In the case of contracts, for example, the official concluding the agreement is neither personally bound nor personally responsible for the consequences of what becomes an organizational act. And
have we not all felt, at some time, a certain *frisson* of irresponsibility
when the will of the group, or the leaders of the group, is allowed to
sway and prevail over valid opposition?

The agent is conceived to act in the interest of his principal. Since
organizations are ostensibly rational interest-pursuing collectivities, it
follows that their acts may conflict with the interests of the next and
higher orders of collectivity within their sphere of operation. The agent
may thus, from time to time, be engaged in doing things of which he or
she would not personally approve under the more liberal conditions of
individual responsibility; in an extrapolation, as it were, from the lawyer who is aware of seeking the exculpation of a guilty client. Or the
group ordained by the organization's structure may have arrived at a
decision to which the administrator is opposed on idiographic value
grounds, but which it seems, on nomothetic value grounds, must be
advanced and executed. The organizational decision is made, according to Barnard, "non-personally from the point of view of its organizational effect and its relation to the organization purpose."[9] Simon's
corresponding positivistic text is "decisions in private management
must take as their ethical premises the objectives that have been set for
the organization."[10] But this appearance of ethical neutrality can serve
as a cover for Type III malice, spite and animus, within and outside the
organization, at the same time that positive morality of the Type I order
can be made to seem irrelevant. And the appearance of rationality can
serve to excuse most, if not all, of the well-documented record of
personally felt injustices at the hands of bureaucracy. Not every anti-
bureaucratic sentiment can be explained away under the term "bureau-
ticism", that special kind of neuroticism which is aggravated by any
kind of nomothetic demand or imposition.[11] Organizational dehuman-
ism or inhumanism extends even to those organizations which by
definition are Type I collectivities: the Roman Catholic church with its
religious purpose, the Communist state with its ideological purpose.

The "system" devalues value. All in the cold light of reason and the cool detachment of agency.

The philosopher Ladd pursued this line of reasoning to the point where he concluded that social decisions cannot be moral:

> Thus, for logical reasons it is improper to expect organizational conduct to conform to the ordinary principles of morality. We cannot and must not expect formal organizations, or their representatives acting in their official capacities, to be honest, courageous, considerate, sympathetic, or to have any kind of moral integrity. Such concepts are not in the vocabulary, so to speak, of the organizational language-game. (We do not find them in the vocabulary of chess either!) Actions that are wrong by ordinary moral standards are not so for organizations; indeed, they may often be required. Secrecy, espionage and deception do not make organizational action wrong; rather they are right, proper and, indeed, rational, if they serve the objectives of the organization. They are no more or no less wrong than, say, bluffing is in poker. From the point of view of organizational decision-making they are "ethically neutral."[12]

This is a restatement from the perspective of moral philosophy of the constantly recurring dilemma in administrative studies which, following Getzels and Guba, we have referred to above as the nomothetic-idiographic dialectic. It is paradoxical that though morality governs relations with others, it is itself an individual matter.

In the analysis of value, we have identified this dilemma as a contest between discipline and indulgence and, throughout, I have implied that the leader should identify with the collective interest. This ethical implication now needs to be emended, sophisticated. It holds good only with qualifications. Here, for example, it is being suggested that organizations are not necessarily benevolent nor forces for social good, but may even be corrupters of their members and their agents, that actions that are wrong by ordinary moral standards are not so for organizations.

The administrator's proclivity for the nomothetic must be morally grounded and have sophisticated justifiability. I do not contest Ladd's analysis of the moral problem; on the contrary, I would lend some strength to his vision of organizations as morally stultifying and ethically dangerous entities, but I would take issue with any underestimation of the administrator as an agent incapable of altering the moral climate and moral destiny of an organization. The power to do this may

not be what one would wish, but there is always the golden potentiality. If the administrator denies that potential by adopting the persona
of the agent, he or she offends as Pontius Pilate then and the positivistic
bureaucrat now, and becomes the organization's faceless creature instead of its creator, a functionary in the lowest sense of the word. Yet, to
fuse individual morality with social decision is difficult; it demands
much, as Barnard constantly stressed, in the way of moral complexity.
In comprehending this complexity, it is necessary to cope with two
difficult concepts: self-interest and responsibility. The first is only
simple on the surface. The administrator has to get clear about his or
her own deepest interests and where they ramify and lie. To do this
calls for much insight, some intuition, and if not, Guardian-style, the
vision of the form of the Good, then at least something of the Pauline
vision, through a glass darkly, of one's own true self.

The second concept, responsibility, is vexed and tortuous and
must be unravelled. We have already raised the question, When *all* are
responsible who *is* responsible? Let us try now to elucidate the notion
of responsibility.

It is first necessary to distinguish between legal, formal, and moral
responsibility. The concept is also vacuous without the connective
linguistic particles, "to" and "for". Responsibility is always *to* some-
body *for* something. The subtlety is that the some*body* may be oneself
and the some*thing* may be an internal phenomenological event.

We shall not be concerned with the causative sense of the term,
e.g., when I accidently trip and in falling break the china vase. I am here
the efficient material cause of a series of entailed consequences which
are unhappy in their outcome. The owner may hold me responsible for
the damaged crockery, but the sense is trivial; we shall interpret moral
responsibility as requiring the condition of some element of voluntarism or free will.

To return to legal responsibility: in this sense, both bodies human
and bodies corporate are held accountable for their acts to a system of
game rules as established by law or legal system—local, national or
international, My accidental breakage of your vase may, of course,
oblige me to recompense you with damages, depending upon the circumstances and the legal game within which we are players. The only
moral element here is any sense of obligation I may happen or choose
to have. The law game-rules will usually, however, trace their origin to
and seek their foundation in Type II consensus values and Type I
principles.

The difficulty in the present context of argument has to do with
bodies corporate. That one cannot hang a common seal has often been
stated, and it is clear that corporate acts cannot always be reduced to

the acts of individuals. If I own ten shares in General Motors I am not responsible if it violates any anti-trust rules, or does those things which are not good for the nation. And if it goes bankrupt I am not financially responsible beyond the rules of legal limited liability, even if the greatest individual economic hardships are a consequence. On the other hand, accountability of a sort can be impressed upon the individual actors who are agents of a corporate body through such legal devices as fines, imprisonment and loss of license. Law has the sanctions of naked power. The force of legal responsibility is real enough, especially since the corporate agents are usually administrators, but it is distinctive from moral responsibility.

Formal responsibility can be considered as a subset of legal responsibility, and refers to the accountabilities sanctioned by the game rules of an organization. Acts are constrained by a potent system of rewards and punishments, including salaries, promotion, demotion and termination. The monitoring functions of administration and management are a part of this responsibility system. And, just as law seeks a ground in societal values, so the system of formal responsibility seeks its ground in the organizational values and policy. Again, the organizational parallel to corporate bodies would be found in those group acts (group decisions) stemming from group processes and structures (committees, boards and ad hoc groups) established formally within the organization. So, if a committee of peers decides by secret vote, or unrecorded consensus, that a colleague should be dismissed, against whom can the injured party point a finger? The popularity of committee action is understandable. It can be a way of responsibly avoiding responsibility. But the responsibility then avoided would be moral responsibility.

This last, moral responsibility, can reduce to the individual only. It is uniquely phenomenological. It is the responsibility of a person to himself for his adherence to his entire range of values but especially to those Type I values with which he has become authentically engaged. It is the ultimate sense of responsibility.

Morality, Moral Complexity, and Leadership

The notion of morality described above is self-referent and psychologically complex. It suggests the presence of internal factors such as conscience and will, and internal dialectical tensions between principles and preferences. This self-centeredness should not be allowed to obscure the fact that the content of moral discourse is outside the individual, and conventionally treats of relationship with others. The disciplines of ethics and moral philosophy are relevant to our understanding of responsibility in so far as they can clarify concepts, set out the arguments, and make the case for Type I and II value. Their function is also to persuade and conduce to moral behavior. They are, as it were, ancillary to moral action. They are not prerequisites of responsibility, but rather aids to moral navigation.

In the administrator's purlieu, the moral actor finds value difficulties magnified in a special way, for here one is not, so to speak, entirely one's self. Technically and officially the administrator is a role incumbent. If we construe this fact as a reduction of personal responsibility, it opens the way for the criticisms of agency and bureaucracy given above. But the administrator, for one, is not a faceless agent, a depersonalized role incumbent. At least four conditions amplify and compound the moral complexity of the task: the administrator (1) designs and creates roles, for him or her self as well as for others; (2) has the overall charge of reconciling the nomothetic and idiographic aspects of the organization; (3) determines, in part or in whole, the organizational values, and (4) must do all this within the constraints imposed by the metavalues (chapter 5). Consider, too, that this role embraces such activities as settling value disputes among organization members, determining the organizational language game, negotiating with levels of interest outside the organization; it requires sometimes a statesman, sometimes a philosopher, sometimes a judge.

In the face of this, Barnard recognized and stressed the need for moral skills. His definition of morals is "personal forces or propensities of a general and subtle character in individuals which tend to inhibit, control, or modify inconsistent immediate specific desires, impulses, or interests, and to intensify those which are consistent with such propensities." When such morals were "strong and stable" there would exist a "condition of responsibility."[13] The translation of values into action, however, rather than their existence in the abstract, is his primary concern, and he illustrates:

> I know men whose morals as a whole I cannot help believe to be lower ethically than my own. But these men command my attention and sometimes my admiration because they adhere to their codes rigidly in the face of great difficulties; whereas I observe that many others who have a 'higher' morality do not adhere to their codes when it would apparently not be difficult to do so. Men of the first class have a higher sense of responsibility than those having, as I view them, the higher ethical standards. *The point is that responsibility is the property of an individual by which whatever morality exists in him becomes effective in conduct.* (Barnard's italics)[14]

I would not wish to contest this, but would draw attention to the operative phrase "whatever morality exists in him." The demands of administrative life can be responded to in different ways, and the response will be a function of the moral substance of the actor. The administrator is also in a special position, having more scope than the ordinary member for the creation and acceptance of the leader role. This, too, will depend upon the leader's moral complexity and sense of responsibility, upon the "morality that exists in him." To some extent the moral sights can be raised or lowered, but even if the value structure within is set, the moral act of consistency with that structure is, in the last analysis, private and personal.

I now wish to make a general hypothesis—one which would be difficult, though not impossible, to test. It is that the quality of leadership is functionally related to the moral climate of the organization and this, in turn, to the moral complexity and skills of the leader. Leadership, as presently understood, is commonly regarded as having three main dimensions: consideration for the followership, production emphasis, and situational factors. I would postulate a fourth dimension; the morality that exists within the leader. This, I suggest, can become subtly externalized, contributing to the administrative phenomena of legitimacy, credibility, and even charisma (where Type I attachments are notably evident). It can on occasion infuse organizational life with a quality of meaning going beyond the nomothetic to the most human and the transrational; it can be, in plain language, inspiring. Yet this aspect of leadership goes unresearched and unexplored at the level of social science.

One is left with the conviction that great schools, great institutions of learning are, in infinitely subtle and complex ways, the reflection and manifestation of the moral integrity of their leaders. The Eton of one headmaster is not the Eton of another, nor the Harvard of today the Harvard of tomorrow. The differences cannot be explained by social science; they rest on the most profound of human subtleties. Yet all this complexity reduces in the end to a chemistry of morality or to an alchemy of values, to praxis.

Options

In assessing the philosophical options facing the educational leader it will not do to be doctrinaire. Nor will it serve any very useful purpose to encode the various value orientations under labels such as realism, pragmatism, progressivism, essentialism and so on. Conventional labels have their uses, but it is probably only in the very rare case that the round executive peg will fit itself firmly into the square philosophical slot. Moreover, I have tried to avoid systematizing, choosing instead to regard philosophical activity as the business of continuous logical and valuational critique. There may be some agreement on the logical side of this business, but there is much less on the valuational side. Besides, the former may be open to inspection, but the latter sealed from view. This need not be a bad thing; the privacy of values may be legitimate even in the public office, but in any event, there is no real means of enforcing their openness to public inspections. Where this book seeks to persuade, however, is in the ethical necessity of raising the private consciousness of value—with the end of advancing authenticity amongst administrators. This authenticity I have defined in no very original way, but in strict accordance with Barnard, and for that matter with Polonius in Hamlet, as being true to one's own set of values, whatever they may be. Authenticity, then, is the submission to the discipline of "whatever morality exists within".

To be sure, this implies some kind of act of faith. One must believe, in a loosely articulated sort of way, that consciousness or, to be more precise, heightened self-consciousness, is good, and will lead to the right, either by evolutionary beneficence or by personal character development. I confess to this transrational element and the reader should be cautioned about it if not against it. The self-consciousness of value implies, perhaps even entails, the self-critique of values, and this, I suggest, leads out of any self-righteous dogmatism or equally self-righteous scepticism towards an active search for individual worth. This philosophical activity seems especially deserving of recommendation in cultural times which are characterized by pluralism, moral relativism, and blind ideological commitment when, to quote Yeats, "The best lack all conviction, while the worst are full of passionate intensity."

It may help in our initial charting of this work to sketch in the extremes of position which presently exist in the field of administration. Let us try as best we can to avoid emotive labels. At one extreme, then, we can expect to find, in the value sense, non-commitment or even painstaking detachment. The administrator may feel that the philosophers as a whole are non-persuasive and may ground himself as best as possible upon the facts or what seem to be the facts, perhaps supporting this position by enlisting the findings of organization theory. Plato would express it this way:

> ... Suppose a man was in charge of a large and powerful animal, and made a study of its moods and wants; he would learn when to approach and handle it, when and why it was expecially savage or gentle, what the different noises it made meant, and what tone of voice to use to soothe or annoy it. All this he might learn by long experience and familiarity, and then call it a science, and reduce it

to a system and set up to teach it. But he would not really know which of the creature's tastes and desires was admirable or shameful, good or bad, right or wrong; he would simply use the terms on the basis of its reactions, calling what pleased it good, what annoyed it bad. He would have no rational account to give of them, but would call the inevitable demands of the animal's nature right and admirable, remaining quite blind to the real nature of and difference between inevitability and goodness, and quite unable to tell anyone else what it was....[15]

At the other end of the continuum, the administrator may be publicly or privately persuaded; or "engaged". One must now name names, though only for the purpose of illustration. These values may be governed by a system of beliefs to which the leader has acceded, such as (say) the purportedly rational doctrine of Marxism or the non-rational religion of Christianity (*credo quia absurdum*) or the commitment to success-through-work, or the conviction that John Dewey or the existentialists have the truth on education. It does not matter what, so long as there are dominant values, principles of the Type I order, which serve to structure and inform the subordinate values in the individual's hierarchy.

The distinction between the extremes of detachment and engagement is a qualitative one, psychological as well as philosophical in nature, whereby in one the will is exercised to refrain from commitment and in the other to embrace it. I would suggest, however, that it is only in technological fantasy or science fiction that a person can achieve any real degree of value neutrality. What is a more realistic continuum, then, is one of sorts or congeries of values ranging from hedonistic individualism through conventionalism to the adoption of principles and systems which extend interest beyond the primitive ego. The value paradigm applies, of course, to the analysis of individual values: happiness at Type III might be conceived as a surplus of private pleasure, at Type II as Benthamite utilitarianism, the greatest good of the greatest number, and at Type I as some form of love and self-transcendence. If we had the time or the patience for such an exercise, we could also classify and locate within this hierarchy of valuation the various labelled packages of philosophy and the much more numerous and realistic aggregates of daily administrative eclecticism, rational and irrational, including perhaps the *arthasastra* and the *via aurea mediocritas*.

Associated with the philosophical positions are psychological complexes of attitudes and value orientation. Kafka's bureaucrats appear as faceless and disengaged, while Weber's are postulated as impartially benevolent. The administrator who has failed either the organization or personally may linger on to serve time, doing only the things necessary to maintain the position and its perquisites, thus moving to the disengaged end of the spectrum. At the other extreme are the involved, the engaged, the committed, the fanatical. It could be argued that both extremes are dangerous: the one leading to apathy, anomie and ineffectiveness, the other to ruthlessness and the enforcement of will by the leader on the led.

The extremes also appear in the administrative literature in the guise of Theory X and Theory Y and the stereotypes of organizational man that we have already discussed. It is my view that both Theory X and Theory Y give valid but partial perspectives. Both present a face of the larger truth, which is more complex and ineluctable. The administrator must take as a first premise the model of human nature expressed in Theory X and then must search for a sophistication of it which would incorporate the insights of Theory Y. Such a synthetic Theory Z would envision man as a complex of lower and higher hierarchically ordered aspirations: an end in himself and the ultimate resource for collective organizational life, finding fulfillment in work-life and in society, but perhaps having to withdraw from the collective embrace in order to win to those spiritual satisfactions which might constitute his or her greatest endeavor. Yet this creature comes trailing no clouds of glory, but all the impedimenta of personal indulgence: selfishness, hedonic myopia, and infinite corruptibility. If there is a logical contradiction in this picture and it does not hang well together, my defense is that neither doe human nature ifself, and neither do organizations.

Theory Z, of course, is speculative. Its pragmatic verification would be by way of the daily experience and insights of practical administration. It would have to be forged in the heat of action and the cool of administrative reflection. To the extent that it is complex, it invokes a corresponding complexity of morality.

Because the administrator is isolated in the formal leader role from organizational fellows and because of the facts of power and hierarchy, his or her particular view of man, of philosophy, carries extra weight. Philosophy is not the prerogative of the professional philosophers but the birthright of all people, and it is certain that the organizational leader will have a philosophy in the sense of a more or less conscious set of loosely or tightly articulated value propositions about the individual, about human beings, and about one person in relation to another. The degree of their coherence, clarity and consistency would be the systematic measure of their quality, and they would constitute administrative philosophy, as distinct from any other sort, to the extent that they addressed the concepts discussed in these pages. I have argued that the administrator has a special onus to do this kind of philosophizing and have suggested that there might be leadership advantages in taking on the task.

In the formal role of leader, a separation occurs. What is created is a leader-follower relation pervaded by values. In my view, the authenticity of the leader stems first from the quality of private commitment to a personal set of values (and these cannot be too divergent from the overall complex of organizational purpose and interest) and second, from the relating of these values to the followership. How is this second thing done? Primarily, I suspect, from the insights generated through sensitive participation, observation, interaction and reflection; by human and humane intercourse. This need not return us to the paragon fallacy nor to the cult of leadership that goes with it. No spectacular behavior is entailed by these suggestions. There are plenty of occasions when, in fact, the best leadership will be followership and when the initiatives will arise elsewhere. But the leader's relationship to the led must be at all times authentic. And I would seek to persuade that, if it is to be thus, the individual must be recognized as being at base intrinsically valuable, an end-in-himself.

It is paradoxical that this essentially Kantian position can be interpreted so as to lead to the administrative norm of universal impartiality on the one hand, and to Marxian hive ethics and the supremacy of the collectivity over the individual on the other hand. My own reading would stress the deep-seated radical "at base" character of intrinsic human worth. The individual is an end-in-himself only, as it were, at the *end*—in those situations where he or she is thrust against the very limits of phenomenological reality. Short of this, perhaps Kant and the Marxists are right. But this very proviso alters the whole coloring and cast of any ethical system which seeks to elevate Type II values to the Type I dimension.

The Continuum of Interest

There is a continuum which cuts across all the options postulated so far. To draw it we take as our basic premise the primacy of self-interest. The ego is then our point of initiation and the line of interest extends from that point outwards to indicate ever larger and wider ranges of interest: extended ego in the family, kin-group and clan; the work-group; the organization of major employment; the community of work and of leisure, the sub-culture; and finally to society, nation, and culture at large. At each discernible quantum shift along this continuum, conflicts of interest can occur. This is well exemplified in an old Sanskrit dictum[16] which can be adapted as follows: "For the sake of the family sacrifice the individual, for the sake of the community sacrifice the family, for the sake of the nation sacrifice the community, for the sake of the world sacrifice the nation, and for the sake of the individual soul sacrifice the whole world." There is a profundity in this wisdom because, while it declares the simple rule of subordination of lesser to larger interests (referred to previously as the nomothetic bias), it also suggests that there is a point at which the intrinsic worth of the individual becomes prior, that is, the individual by virtue of the quality of being an end-in-himself usurps and preempts the nomothetic rule. In our scheme, such points could only occur at the Type I level of value and it follows in the practical logic of administration that they were best avoided.

The continuum of interest, with its extremes of ego definition, can, however, serve a useful purpose as a skeletal structure upon which the administrator can fashion a private philosophy. We have seen previously how a nomothetic bias is appropriate to administrative value systems. It was then argued that this presumptive bias must be tempered by the value complexities arising from given situations and the administrator's own moral complexity and philosophy of human nature. It is futile to wish with Plato for the advent of the philosopher kings, but it is neither unreasonable nor impractical to seek programs which will move leaders in the Platonic direction. Any such program would acknowledge the continuum of interest and would entail at least the following stages.

First, one would seek the self-knowledge of one's own values by private reflection, including to the best of one's ability the scrutiny of personal metavaluational assumptions and constraints. Second, one would review, in the manner outlined above, the metavalues of one's organization and then the overt scope of the organizational values proper. Third, the leader would analyze for conflict points the extension of the organizational interest into the social, national and cultural environment and, lastly, would seek to become as aware as possible of the scope of personal self-interest, now redefined as extended ego in the organization, and in familial and affective connections. If this contemplative activity does not yield any consciousness of irreconcilable conflict, then no more need immediately be done and there will already have been a gain in self-awareness and sophistication.

When value conflict does occur, as it most certainly will, in the ordinary run of organizational life, its resolution can be approached through use of our value model. The values which are involved are first analyzed in terms of type or level and then decided or settled on the postulate of hierarchy, at the lowest level of resolution consistent with authenticity and moral responsibility.

All these elements—value type, authenticity, responsibility—are relative to factual situations, but converge ultimately upon an extremity. At the point of extremity, the end of the continuum of interest is reached and the ultimate test of administrative integrity is encountered. Though it be harsh to say, at such a point it might indeed be necessary to "sacrifice the whole world." It is somewhat understandable, therefore, that the undertaking of administrative philosophy can engender some hesitancy and reluctance and must be approached with great caution. One must have the faith that ignorance is not bliss and that "Know Thyself" is a rewarding precept.

There is another, perhaps less philosophical and more psychological, way of expressing these general ideas. We can make use of the concepts of discipline and commitment. The essence of administrative morality could then be thought of as twofold: first, the conscious commitment to the highest level of interest proper to one's personality and personal situation (as determined by self value anaylsis) and, second, the discipline of translating the resultant values into action and being constrained by them in action. The psychological terms which call for greater clarification, analysis and understanding are primarily those of discipline and commitment, but would certainly include detachment, compartmentalization, fulfillment, self-identification, self-actualization, and power. To the practical administrator, the blurring of disciplinary lines between the fields of philosophy and psychology is not a matter of the first importance—simply use whatever means or metaphors serve best in the analysis of the continuum of interest.

Administrative discretion occurs when the ends of policy are unclear, or when the ends are clear but in contention by opposing interests. The first case is well illustrated in public education. Administrators may make inconsistent decisions in this area, but because of the vagueness of policy guidelines the inconsistencies can pass unnoticed. In this type of situation, the demands of moral complexity, knowing when to raise issues of principle and when to avoid them, can be intensified, and the temptation to resolve issues at the pragmatic or lower levels may be greatly persuasive. The problem is further compounded by the fact that two types of administrator, professional and political, are engaged in the *de facto* making of policy.

In the case when ends are clear but in opposition, the administrator has the problem of divergent objectives and contending parties. The complication here is to ensure that all the values and all the types or levels of value relevant to the case are entered into the conscious deliberations, since opposing parties will seek to conceal or disguise them where this is thought to be advantageous. Thereafter, the decision whether to press for resolution by (say) victory on one side or compromise (Type I *vs.* Type IIb) would be the second order value judgment, with all its attendant implications. The desirability of the administrator's having a rich personal value structure and commensurate value skills is very clear. The question to be raised is whether this is best left to informal chance, or whether the odds of its occurring can be improved by some formality or training.

Of course, this entire work strongly suggests the need for moral and values education at the executive level. It seeks, itself, to contribute in some way to that cause.

Now let us consider things more personally. How am I to go about value praxis? How can I make praxis a practical reality for myself?

Value Auditing

A value audit is a stock-taking of one's own values. It is a reflective and contemplative effort which seeks to bring into the light of consciousness the range, depth and breadth of one's preferences, conditioning and beliefs. It can be done hypothetically, that is, apart from considerations of any particular case or problem, but more typically, and more importantly, it is done with a specific focus on a praxis problem which is being faced in a real situation.

The analysis should be as sophisticated as possible within the factual constraints of time pressure and commitments. It should not be a mere back-of-the-envelope calculus of pros and cons followed by lightning closure and impulsive action. Indeed, closure should be withheld until the threshold of inner certainty is passed or, if that is not possible, at least until there is a sense of inner confidence that the best judgments have been made. When the audit is conducted about a specific problem, the following questions must be asked:

1. What *are* the values in conflict in the given case? Can they be named?
2. What *fields* of value (V_1 through V_5) are most affected or most salient?
3. *Who* are the value actors?
4. How is the conflict distributed interpersonally and intrapersonally?
5. Is the conflict interhierarchical or intrahierarchical on the value paradigm? (e.g., Is a Type I value in conflict with a Type IIa? Or are divergent Type III values in contest?)
6. Are ends seeking to dictate means? Or are means subverting ends?

7. Could the conflict be apparently resolved by removing a value actor or group of actors?
8. What are the *Metavalues?*
9. Is there a principle (Type I value) which must be invoked or can that be avoided?
10. Can the conflict be resolved at a lower level of the paradigm?
11. Can the tension of non-resolution be avoided? (That is, must the conflict be resolved now?)
12. What rational and pragmatic consequences follow from possible and probably scenarios?
13. What bodies of value consensus and political relevance are involved, both within and without the organization?
14. To what extent does one have control over the formative and informative media in the case (press, radio, television, lines of communication, informal organization, etc.)?
15. How does one analyze the state of affect, and affect *control,* amongst the parties to the case?
16. What is the analysis of commitment? (Using the paradigm).
17. What is the interest of the commons, the collectivity? How can higher level interest be invoked? And how high need one go?
18. What, in the end, is *my true will* in the case before me?

It is the careful reflection upon such questions prior to administrative action that constitutes the hallmark and warrant of leadership responsibility. It can, of course, be at once admitted that the audit can never be either fully exhaustive or fully conducted. Life is short and art is long, as Goethe remarks. But the administrator is not always in the field of battle and the heat of combat. That there is some time for reflection is proven by the fact that the reader, having come this far, is now at these words. And organizations endure, according to Barnard, in proportion to the breadth of the morality by which they are governed.[17]

Perversely, it is the very nature of the emotional (Type III) side of our being to avoid this kind of responsibility. The press to instantaneous gratification combined with the urges to closure and action—sometimes defended as decisiveness—conduces to our avoidance of the value audit, to bad praxis and irresponsibility. In this lies the heart of the problem of administrative morality. Value auditing, on the other hand, sensitizes both the pragmatic leader to the importance of principle and the ideological leader to the corresponding importance of pragmatics.

Illustrations from organizational life are plentiful enough. Prototypical decisions of hiring, firing and promotion may be at best Type IIa

for the leader but for the affected party they may be Type I. This interhierarchical conflict may easily be overlooked. That a middle-aged
employee is about to lose all career prospects through some highly
rational realignment of organizational structure may go inadequately
assessed or not be assessed at all. At the very least the decision maker
should be aware of the interhierarchical value conflict that exists. And
by what maxim is it to be decided? Is the integrity of the affected individual sufficiently at stake to justify the subversion of the apparently
larger interest of the nomothetic collectivity? Is it, *pace* Kant, that the
individual ceases to be a means to an end and has become an end in
himself? Or is it a case for straight-out tough-mindedness and "moral
ruthlessness," with the leader as the moral equivalent of surgeon? The
value audit does not lead easily to the answers to value questions, but
at least it provides a safeguard for the ultimate protection of humane
values in an organization.

The final phase of the value audit is action. This includes the possibility of inaction since, logically, the latter is merely negative action.
Action necessitates the employment of power, authority and influence
and, for the leader especially, the commitment of will. Implicit also in
this is the employment, where necessary, of the whole armamentarium
of the *arthasastra* when action is directed to the resolution of value disputes. If Type I values are not engaged, then one can hope for value
change to follow upon value action, however grudgingly and slowly.
One may also expect realignments of interest patterns in the fields of
value action and predictable shifts in the continuous flux of political
consensus. The leader is sensitive to and monitors all this. On the other
hand, no such comfortable evolution of value change is to be expected
if Type I values come into conflict. It must be remembered that power
(in the last analysis *force*) can alter relationships and events without
altering values. The international arena (Ireland, Poland, the Middle
East) is replete with examples of this intractability. It can be said of
value problems at this level of systematics that they are never solved,
however they be forcibly resolved. They are insoluble though resolv-
able.

Such problems erupt from time to time within the lesser systems
of organizational life. It then becomes the onus of leadership to subject
them to analysis, monitoring and audit. The analysis of any problem
cannot but enhance the prospects for its *resolution in praxis*.

Emotional Control

The leader has to do two things. First, analyze and continue to
monitor the level of affect in the followership—all part of a general obligation to know the human side of the organization. The second, and

more difficult, is to analyze and monitor his or her own affect, to "know thyself."

If the leader is volatile, labile, impulsive, it may be that the finest analysis, the most thorough-going audit, is cast aside and an impulse, affectively driven and acted upon, can lead untold organizational actors to uncalculated calamities. Analysis in itself is merely academic if not complemented by right action which, in turn, may depend upon adequate emotional control on the part of the leadership. Praxis is always a function of the leader's affective state.[18] It is especially important to be aware of the dark side of personality, which acts so as to weaken will and frustrate the commitment to values. Emotion in this sense is a sort of loss of consciousness, a sleep of the conscience, moral impotence.

Philosophically speaking, the formal leader has a specialist function in that he or she is expected to gain a position of value perspective which affords a degree of detachment, non-attachment and affective disinterest different from and greater than that to be expected in other organizational roles. The leader is expected to perceive the total organizational situation in a clear-eyed and cool-headed way. This is an obligation of perspective and affect control which is quite apart from the leader's personal complex of interests. Value analysis itself presupposes this, but there are obstacles to this desideratum. The administrator is human and shares in the normal human endowment of imperfection, including the ebb and flow of affective impulse. This range of crude affective reaction to situational stimuli runs all the way from panic to insensitivity. Primal motivations are continually being triggered or inhibited, occasionally indulged. Such emotive response is free-floating and decathected. It is crude and primal, directly related to ancestral instincts to fight, freeze, or flee. This generalized and prepotent complex of affect can be logically subsumed under the principle of self-preservation if that principle is taken to include the impulse to sexual gratification encompassed in the Freudian notion of the id. Affect of this kind has not yet attached itself to implicit or explicit values as concepts of the desirable. It does not yet invest particular values, but it has motivating force nonetheless and can be a powerful behavioral determinant, even through the simple dynamism of forcing the actor to seek relief from the anxiety or tension which it generates.

It is a large part of the leader's search for self-knowledge to be aware of one's private potential for this type of response to stimuli. The leader is always obliged to have it under control, a responsibility neither easy nor simple, for doing must here be subordinated to being. The light of consciousness must not be extinguished by the tides of affect that can surge within the psyche. Rather those tides, and the force and energy they represent, must be sublimated and placed at the service of consciousness itself. Not easy? But who ever said leadership was?

Values and Reality

Our investigation of value praxis has led us inexorably inwards. As Doris Lessing once remarked, "In the end there is no place to travel but in." All this introspection may cause some uneasiness; especially as the world of action, in education as elsewhere, is a world of extroversion. But we must remember that the root and source of all true action is inner. Outer stimuli can of themselves at best result in *re*action. Greenfield speaks most cogently of the essential innerness of social reality and deserves to be quoted at length.

First, organizations are people—nothing beyond them, nothing less. Organizations are in people; they are not out there. It is possible and, indeed, necessary to speak of the concept of organization. We make a major error if we think of that concept as representing a natural entity existing beyond human action and subject to human control only by the mastery of laws that govern natural entities of all kinds. The alternative theory must recognize that organization lies in the personal and the human; it lies in self. It lies in the creativity of the self, in its constrained freedom, and in its capacity to choose. Organization lies also in the power of the self to make the world around conform—though it will do so imperfectly—to the desires of self and to its will. Expression of self needs other people, but it will necessarily oppose other people as well. The central questions of administration must therefore address not only how people do relate to each other but how they ought to. Education is a deeply moral enterprise. How can the administration of such an enterprise be any the less moral?

Secondly, organizations are social inventions. They are like the theatre, all artifice. We go to the theatre to see a play about life. The lights dim and the curtain rises. We know that these are actors we see, playing roles. Yet we go along with the trick and will ourselves to believe; we suspend our disbelief, so that we can be entertained, enlightened, and sometimes deeply moved. We make theatre into life by believing the illusion before us. More importantly, we also make life into theatre by believing that illusion. What we recognize as organization is a constructed reality, a social invention, and an illusion.

Organization is not a system, a structure, or a need-fulfilling device. It is a constructed social reality or illusion that is made by people and maintained by them. Organization has no power to act beyond the action of specific, concrete individuals. The capacity of people to construct their world and then regard it as independent and objective explains why illusion and reality are often the same thing in social affairs.

In the alternative theory, administrators are active, interested and wilful; in some sense both they and others involved with them know what they are doing. Organization is another word for people living their lives in context with other people. An environment, of course, is another word for organization. While the physical world is out there (as far as we can tell), the social environment is in other people, even as organizations lie within ourselves.

Fourth, the world of values is inside us, deep inside us. Values are the ultimate subjective reality. They have no presence whatsoever in what we call the objective world, though some people believe deeply (another value) that they are God-given. Because organizations are people bearing their own meaning and trying to impose them on others, our organizations are suffused with values and they, too, are inevitably and irretrievably subjective.

This journey in search of an understanding of organization and administration ends with a consideration of values—the ultimate subjective reality. What now becomes clear is that it is impossible to consider values in organization and administration if these entities are built on theoretical foundations that separate them from human purpose and human action. Values can appear in organizational action and reality only if the individual too has a place there. To allow the individual into theory about organizations and administration requires an acknowledgement of the individual's perspective and subjective appreciation of reality, for these are the only grounds in which values exist. We cannot find them in the natural world around us, only the non-natural order that people create and in the beliefs, attitudes, and appreciation of self and others that shaped the formation of that order.

Education is a deeply mysterious process. So also are organization and administration. In none of these fields should we settle for a theory that is obviously inadequate to understand the basic realities it deals with.[19]

But education, organization and administration are not merely mysterious. They are not intractable; they are art forms. That education is an art has been argued in the first chapter of this book, but that organization and administration are in the aesthetic domain of artistry is less commonly recognized. A Japanese industrialist expresses it this way:

> The administrator's task is equally creative. He, too, [like the artist] starts with a blank slate. In setting up a business, he first formulates basic policy, decides where to get capital and how to obtain manpower, what kind of factories to build, what to produce, how to go about production, and how to sell. From nothing he creates something complex, adding one element to the picture at a time. As in art, close attention must be given to the overall effect so that the proper balance can be maintained among the elements. Administration produces something from nothing through the constant exercise of human ingenuity. Moreover, the creation process is never-ending, for its various facets must be maintained and improved continually. If a sufficient balance is achieved in the administration of a complex business the enterprise is vibrant with the spirit of its leader, and the observer is moved to applaud what has been created. I believe that leadership, in essence, is an artistic endeavour to which high intrinsic value should be attached.[20]

enterprise of education. Here the aim is to create from the plastic raw material of developing human minds the qualities and characters that will populate and determine the future of our kind—art not for the sake of art but for the sake of humanity. What higher art form can there be than this; the moral art of educational leadership?

We have now made an expansive but abstract survey of this value-laden art. Let us see what conclusions and what prescriptive or practical implications can be drawn.

7

Prescriptions and Practicalities

At the beginning of this book we examined the claim that education was in some way special and reached the conclusion that the institution of education was special by virtue of its generality of purpose and its humaneness or overriding concern with the total human condition. That is, it was distinguished by its moral aspect. Education both serves us by providing the means of livelihood and as the very end of that livelihood. To the question, "Why are we here?" can be answered, "To become educated." No other institution or complex organization attends to the *general* aims of life in quite the same way. Hospitals are humane organizations and medicine is a humane institution, but they attend specifically to the ills and repairs of the physical body. The institution of religion concerns itself with the spiritual aspect of life. Industry, trade and commerce subserve the economic side of living, military and police the security side, and so on. Only education attempts, in manifold ways, to deal with all values: economic, aesthetic, and liberal. These manifold ways include the multiversity, the one-room school, the conservatory of the arts, the museum, the educational television network, the book and pen, the comprehensive high school, the ministry of education, the infinity of technical and human modes in which education is conceived and delivered. But no matter how specialized or subdivided the organizational unit, the cachet of the overall mission of education attaches to it in some measure. And that measure applies to and is fulfilled or frustrated by the leader of the unit. It can be a fundamental source of motivation and inspiration. That is why educational administrators should frequently consult their philosophical roots. The great project of education in which they participate can be a constantly renewed source of energy and pride.

Nevertheless this great diffuseness and generality of purpose differentiates educational from other organizations in another way. The charge that in education we neither know what we are doing nor where we are going is one which is often laid and is sometimes difficult to deny. Generally speaking, the more abstract the purpose (self-actualization, good citizenship, aesthetic appreciation) the less the educational organization will be like all others; the more the educational purpose is specific (typing and shorthand, automobile mechanics—marketable skills) the more it can be identified with the commonality of organizations and the more educational administration is subject to the general canons of organization and administration theory.

There is, however, another distinguishing feature of education. The border line of any education system is ill-defined because its rank and file members are at one-and-the-same time members and clientele. The students who perform the actual productive work of the organization, namely learning, simultaneously form the lowest level of hierarchy in the organization and are the ultimate consumers of the organization's product. Thus, education dragoons its clientele. By contrast, the rank and file of a government bureaucracy or a manufacturing firm are separate and distinct from the clienteles that they serve. The lines separating the organization from the rest of the world and its member's "us" from its customer's "them" are sharp and clear. Identification is more complex in education. A student may be attracted to a school or college, to the point of emotionally identifying with it through life, but also expects, during the period of active membership at least, to be served by it. And, if need be, parents or guardians will speak for the student in this role of client. This means that the educational leader's responsibility and moral scope are more diffuse than those of non-educational administrative peers. The moral act becomes more difficult. Rarely can the leader retreat to a V_3 position and indulge the luxury of an us-versus-them attitude, for the they, like Mongol invaders, are already within the wall. And yet, paradoxically, a school must erect and defend boundaries between itself and the rest of the world in order to establish its V_1-V_3 identity. It must be, like a home perhaps, both an island and a retreat, but also part of the main.

There is yet another differentiating feature of education. Its product is never tangibly realized. If its product is an alteration in the mind of the client, then that product is intangibly and imponderably implicated in all the future behaviors and experience of the learner. Unquestionably we accept that education affects the future and shapes history, but it is difficult, if not impossible, to assess this qualitative outcome in any quantitative way. Oxford and Eton may enumerate the prime ministers amongst their alumni, but the implied causal connection between education and political success is incommensurate with the relation between, say, agricultural hours worked and crop yield, or, in general, between present input and future output. Graduation from school or college may carry with it a diploma or credential which can be, and usually is, conceived as the product of the student's labors, but the real product is intangible. It is psychological and characterological. That is to say, it is moral. And the relationship between educational organizations and the future of society, devoutly though we may affirm and believe in it, is an unclear relationship.

Education is indeed special, but it also shares, in its administrative aspect, a commonality with all other institutions. If one could run a post office one might not necessarily be able to run a school, but if one could attain to the office of postmaster general one would very likely be able to fill the role of president of a university. Administration is a generalism.[1] The same factors of structure and function apply across widely differing organizational cultures; the same psychological demands of affective control, distancing, and compartmentalization contribute to executive stress; the same moral dilemmas and the same value paradigm apply across the board.

The result of these similarities and differences is the prescription that the generality of administration applies across organizational cultures, but the specificity of those cultures and contexts modulates leadership behavior, emphases and styles. That said, there is one aspect of administrative life in which problem-solving skills are especially transferable from context to context and that is conflict management and conflict resolution. This most vital and essential practicality will be dealt with next.

The Resolution of Conflict

The value paradigm is a conceptual tool which is universally applicable to all affective or valuational phenomena. Its general application to praxis has been discussed in the previous chapter. Now we must consider its use in resolving real conflicts of value in practical contexts. A theory which cannot translate into practice remains academic and tentative. The paradigm however, especially in combination with value audit, can be applied to the most tortuous and vexing of complex controversial issues and conflict. In any real situation, the first question to be settled is this: Is the conflict *inter*hierarchical or *intra*hierarchical in terms of the paradigm? It is unfortunate that such tongue-twisting terminology has to be used but the sense is simply this: Is the value conflict *between* levels in the paradigm? Or are the values in conflict at the *same* level of the paradigm? This necessitates, of course, some preliminary value analysis and also the identification of the conflicting values by labeling them. The decision rules and strategies which might apply in any given case depend upon the answer to this first question.

Interhierarchical Conflict

Here the values in conflict are at different levels of the paradigm. That is, they are different logically—different in kind, not just different in degree.

A Type I value (such as commitment to Catholic dogma and principles) may be in conflict with a Type II value (I like this teacher but I must ask her to resign because she is obtaining a divorce).

Or the Type I may conflict with IIa. (The university must enroll more students to be economically viable [IIa] but this will necessitate a lowering of standards [I].)

Or I versus IIb. (School staff are determined on a withdrawal of extracurricular services as part of contract negotiations [IIb] but this violates the principal's own deep commitment to the provision of these services as a fundamental professional obligation [I].)

The above examples illustrate conflict between Type I and other levels of value, but conflict need not involve level I. Thus the general conflict pattern discussed at length in chapter 4: the problem of the common good *versus* self-interest, or simply the dialectical tension between the idiographic and nomothetic aspects of organization, may appear as conflict between levels III and IIa or III and IIb. (For example, a careerist colleague is seeking promotion [III] which would, on the affective and congnitive evidence, be deleterious to the welfare of the organization [IIa, IIb].)

Or IIa versus IIb. (A faculty committee is dominated by a single-issue political activitist [IIb] and the administrator is convinced this will be harmful to the public perceptions of the college and its staff [IIa].) Another typical example could be taken from the ethical dilemma of whistle-blowing. An administrator or a teacher knows a colleague to be incompetent or to have indulged in some form of of professional malpractice. How then is the value of collegial solidarity (IIb) to be reconciled with the larger interest of organization or its clientele (IIa)?

All these illustrations give examples of identifying the conflict. Having identified the conflict what then is the maxim for its resolution? In general, the ethical maxim is that the lower ranking value should be subordinated to the higher. This was referred to earlier (p. 133), where in its original Sanskrit version the individual was to be sacrificed for the sake of the family; the family for the sake of the community, the community for the sake of the nation, the nation for the sake of the world and, finally, the whole world for the sake of the individual soul. The problem here, of course, is the concept of "soul". In practical terms, it means that the administrator or leader should be willing to apply the rule except where it would cause harm of a gross or spiritual nature to the individual concerned—perhaps in some sense what legal minds might call cruel and unusual harm. Thus, it is conceivable that the loss of a job, for example, might prove utterly destructive to a given individual. In such circumstances the leader might feel ethically justified in using this high level escape clause to abrogate the general logic of primacy of the larger interest. In other words, the leader would reinterpret the larger interest as being that of maintaining the threatened employee's psychological integrity and, in effect, in this value analysis he or she would upgrade the value of continued employment to level I.

This example also illustrates how mechanical maxims, however well founded in ethical doctrine, must yield in the end, in the crucial case, to art—to the leader's moral art. In each moral-ethical situation the executive brings to bear the totality of his or her knowledge of the situation, of the task, of those who are led and of himself or herself. In certain circumstances, this summative knowledge will override the general logic of interhierarchical conflict resolution. The exception to the general rule can here be called The Principle of Most Principle. It may be, in the example given, that the dependant employee should be kept on, the telescope clamped to the blind eye, even if the organizations should be become less efficient and effective thereby. Excellence may well be sacrificed on the altar of humanity at times, or vice versa. The decision is one of moral leadership and a function of the leader's total value knowledge and total values education.

Psychologically speaking, one must add that no amount of value education or experience necessarily ensures the leader a good night's sleep. Thickness of skin, or at least of the membranes between mental compartments, might conduce to that, but the point of moral artistry has nothing to do with the leader's comfort, and everything to do with what is *right*. It is a sad truth that the perception and the reality of unpleasant emotional arousal as a result of personnel decision making and interaction deters many from embarking on a career in educational administration. They are faint-hearted with good reason but they could be courageous with better reason. In the end, the things they may fear all come down to value conflict and the handling of such conflict can be intellectually understood and psychologically mastered.

There is a second exemption to the maxim that lower values must be subordinated to higher ones. We can call it, by contrast, the Principle of Least Principle. This applies when the administrator is capable of negotiating or reducing the level of value conflict among others, always assuming that the leader's own values or those of the organization are not critically engaged. Thus, on a campus where there might be, say, militant political activism, the president might act so as to keep the coalitions as informal as possible and potential controversy a mere matter of individual opinion (III). If coalitions do organize (IIb), he or she may then seek to keep them out of the formal structure as long as possible and, failing this, incorporate them in the formal committee and task force or even line structure (IIa), but only when politically obliged to do so. At all events, the leader will seek to prevent and deter the emergence of Type I value commitments and the consequent arousal of passions or zealotry that they may bring in their wake. The logic here is one of simple conflict reduction and, again assuming the caveat given above that the leader's own values or those of the organization are not at stake, the defensible assumption is that less conflict is preferable to more. That is, the lower on the hierarchy the value issues can be contained, or the "less principle", the better. Resort to the Principle of Least Principle[2] is, however, not always defensible. In the following illustration, for example, it is not properly invoked.

A minister of education approves changes in the system which will involve long-term economic costs (e.g., alterations in teacher bargaining arrangements or provision of costly but popular curriculum changes). These the minister perceives as having the merit of temporarily satisfying all vocal stakeholders and ensuring re-election. Here, political survival (III) and political calm (IIb) are bought at the price of deferred economic costs (IIa). The reason Least Principle does not apply here is that the minister's own values (and those of his party) are engaged. The minister is not detached and a better defense thus might be to argue that the long-term interests necessitate the mid-term losses now being discounted for the short-term gain. Such an argument would take the problem out of between-levels conflict and place it in the within-levels type, which we must now discuss.

Intrahierarchical Conflict

In both kinds of value conflict it is rare in practice for the choice to be clearly between good and evil; rather the norm is one of choosing between good and good. Intrapersonal value conflict is always between positive goods, because no one has any difficulty in choosing good over bad or right over wrong. A value actor, however judged by the outside observer, is always acting in a way which for him or her is right or good. Furthermore, conflict in a choice situation is always between *two* goods. We cannot decide between three or more things. Instead the multiplicity must be reduced must be reduced (by a process of conscious or subconscious rank-ordering) to a final pair of contending values from which one must be selected. This process of reduction is not necessarily easy, as illustrated by the difficulty of choosing wallpaper or fabric colors from a wide range of options. The process of reduction is also illustrated by the common administrative value problem of selecting the winner from a field of eligible and strong candidates. Iteration may be necessary in difficult cases. The wallpaper or candidate rejected at one phase of the selection process may be re-entered into the contest at a later stage if the process appears to be stalling. Over-iteration can, of course, lead to indecisive waffling or even paralysis, enhancing the apparent value dilemma. But ultimately the conflict must be sharpened and narrowed to the point where only two values are contending.

When at level III the contending values—a choice, say, of restaurant or TV channel, of this office furnishing or that—are matters of sheer preference, the resolution rule is simple. The stronger preference wins out. That is, strength of preference is the deciding factor. If all values (as the positivists and determinists argue) could be reduced to this level, then it could be said that all value conflicts are resolved in this way, by a sort of hidden valence vector calculus inaccessible to consciousness. We would not go so far. It is enough to say that in the individual case, conflict between Type III values can be resolved by adequate introspection, the aim of which is to discover the relative strengths of preference. In interpersonal conflict between Type III values, the resolution is again on the basis of strength of preference and the same principle of careful introspection applies. Whoever has the strongest emotive preference wins out. The greatest difficulty of resolution occurs the closer in assessed magnitude the contending values are but, in compensation, the closer they approach equality the less significant the conflict resolution becomes and it can then be settled increasingly on a random basis—the toss of a coin or the roll of a dice determining the winner.

At level IIb the resolution strategy changes. Here we have, for example, such cases as opposing public opinions, voting behavior and group dynamics generally. Suppose a committee is split on a curriculum change or the hiring of a candidate for a position, but agreed on the general cost-benefit analysis of each situation. Suppose, too, that no Type I values are present or at issue. The strategy for conflict resolution then becomes dialectic or, in plain language, talk. The process of resolution must be allowed to persist (and the dialectical tension must be endured) long enough for the parties to the dispute to express themselves and exercise their several powers of persuasion. Thus, strength of preference again operates, but manifests at a group or collective level. This is also referred to sometimes as compromise, but can be more technically described (given a properly free market of contending values) as vector resolution of Type IIb values.

Type IIa conflicts are resolved by cost-benefit analysis. The rational examination of the context for cause-effect chains determines the ultimate perceived or hypothesized outcomes of a choice between, say, investing the pension fund in Plan A or Plan B; or initiating or delaying a building program; or deciding whether to keep open or to close a certain school (assuming that the decision has been elevated above settlement by mere head count or public opinion). That is to say, force of reason or force of logic should be sufficient for answering the question, Which of two Type IIa values is the best value? The problem of course is that our rationality is always bounded or limited. Nevertheless, to the extent that we can pursue analysis, to that extent is the resolution of this type of conflict a straightforward one.

Finally, we come to the severest value problem of all—the rock on which men and nations have broken in the past and will continue to do so in the future: Type I intrahierarchical conflict. How are Type I value disputes resolved? Or even can they be resolved? How does one determine the superior value as opposed to merely reconciling the actors holding contending Type Is? Historical conflicts between Protestant and Catholic, Hindus and Muslims, between the forces of Fascism and Communism, and contemporary struggles between terrorists and established order, between pro-life and pro-choice zealots in the abortion issue, between radicals and reactionaries in education serve as examples. At the individual level of analysis this type of conflict means that a leader may have to choose between career and principles if these latter come into conflict with the principles held with equal vigour by the board of directors or trustees.

All of this, it can be noted, is the stuff of dramatic conflict, of art and literature. But in art, unlike life, resolution is within the creative gift of the author. In life or reality the disappointing analytic answer is that there is no mode of resolution, no maxim, no strategy for determining the "best" value. There is only anguish, dilemma, and powerful negative emotion. The pseudo-solution is provided by history itself, for history in effect appears to resolve these conflicts. The war is won or lost. The leading actors die, are killed or are otherwise removed from the stage. Yet this is resolution without solution. the actual value problem is left unsolved and humankind is none the wiser in the end. That Hitler lost the war does not prove that Fascists values were wrong. Had he won the war we would all now be espousing them and proving thereby that democratic values were wrong. History is an arbiter not a judge. After enough historical process, and quite likely enough bloodletting violence and death, religious and political and ideological factions may come to an accommodation and learn to live, however reluctantly, with each other. The passion which funds Type I

FIGURE 1

Conflict Resolution Logic

Type of Conflict

		Between Levels	Within Levels
Level of Conflict on Paradigm	I	Subordinates All Lower[1] Values	Historical Process[2] (God)
	IIa	Subordinates All Lower Values	Strength of Logic (Analysis)
	IIb	Subordinates All Lower Values	Strength of Persuasion (Dialectic)
	III	Subordinate to All Higher Values	Strength of Preference (Affectivity)

Notes: (1) Between=levels resolution has two exceptions: Principle of Least Principle and Principle of Most Principle.

(2) Type I within=level conflict can be interpreted by believers as resolution through divine intervention.

commitments may spend itself over time and the original values thereby degenerate to level IIa, or lower still, upon the paradigm. The initial charisma that attached to the leader dissipates and the organization, minus zeal, devolves into a rational bureaucratic mode. History ultimately works to defuse this type of conflict, but as often as not by then the explosion has already taken place. And history's retrospective, on Type I value terms, can tell us nothing about the future prospective of Type I values. As Oscar Wilde once said, "A thing is not necessarily true because a man dies for it." Value conflict analysis here comes to a halt. There is no rule. Except it should be the administrative maxim to avoid for as long as possible, or at all if possible, the emergence of this category of value conflict to the extent that it is within the leader's power to do so.

We may now draw the discussion together in the form of a diagram.

Advantages

There are three advantages to using the paradigm in praxis. First, it is universal in application to all administrative value problems. Practice with it leads to proficiency and confident value analysis on the part of the leader. Secondly, it prevents us from committing a common value fallacy, the homogenetic fallacy which occurs when we assume that values are differentiated by degree rather than by kind.[3] (The value of a life, for example, is different for a systems analyst in the Pentagon to what it is for a soldier in the field). Thirdly, it provides us with a relatively neutral conceptual tool which, nevertheless, is capable of expressing the most idealistic systems of ethical thought. The analyst individually determines from the situation what values are at which level of hierarchy. Thereafter the logic of conflict resolution applies as shown.

For all these reasons, paradigmatic analysis is to be recommended. It imports order and knowledge into a domain where otherwise practice may be impulsive, uninformed, inchoate, dangerous, and potentially damaging to self and others. Of itself, of course, the instrument will not transmute leadership from a moral art into a science, but it will certainly enhance the sophistication of that art in whatever directions the leader might wish to take it.

Maxims, Mega and Mini

Since administration is closer to art than to science, it is legitimate for the practical leader to pursue truth after his or her own fashion and to pragmatically adopt rules of thumb, taking maxims from wherever they can be found. Indeed, short of the emergence of full-blown applied organization theory or some form of behavioristic managerial robotics, this is what the leader must do.

The resort to maxims need not, therefore, be considered improper. Each generation inherits from the preceding one and we continue to learn from the past and from the long history of administrative thought. The discipline of educational administration is not a science, although it has its managerial quasi-scientific side and pursues it with intermittent vigor. Human behavior in organizations can be studied empirically, tentative hypotheses can be tested and tentative generalizations made. In the end, however, what tends to remain as I have shown at length elsewhere[4] are propositions and, ultimately, maxims. These constitute a sort of folk-wisdom which ought never to be despised—even when the maxims might appear to be contradictory.[5] Maxims are grounded in experience and can be refined and tempered through the advance of social science and leadership theory. They are intermediate in the hierarchy of knowledge between speculation and guesswork and empirically verifiable assertions with rigorous predictive power. They are propositions-in-use whose value lies in experiential efficacy and the pragmatic testing of ongoing organizational life. The maxims, delivered as practical prescriptions below, fall into two sets: major and minor, or mega and mini. To the limits of my knowledge, they are not contradicted or annulled by theory, philosophy, or research. Moreover, they are grounded in the discussion of the preceding chapters. Their worth however, must rest ultimately with the leader who adopts and employs them.

Megamaxims

1. Know the task.
2. Know the situation.
3. Know the followership.
4. Know oneself.

These have already been introduced (p. 83), but their recapitulation is timely since they constitute the major practical and prescriptive injunctions for the process of leadership conceived as moral art. Note once again that they are knowledge imperatives as well as moral injunctions, and that they are ranked in descending order of difficulty. Everyone in the organization is concerned with definition of task. Such definition may range from the highest level of philosophical abstraction: the single word *Veritas* on the Harvard crest, for example, down to the most elementary level of specificity: What assignment must the student do next to satisfy the course requirements? Purposes, ends, aims, objectives, targets, goals all occur within real historical contexts. The leader must struggle to achieve the auspicious match or fit of task to situation and then must rely upon the followership to carry it out. To do all this entails both a knowledge of human nature in general and the particular human natures embodied in the real organization, formal and informal. The leader can never know enough, but must maximize and optimize what can be known within the reality constraints that he or she faces. Administration cannot be simplistically reduced to either human relations or communication, but these two elements are surely vital to the overall process. Finally, there is the injunction to self-knowledge. This extends above and beyond the organization, and before and after, as well as during, the leader's commitment to it. Morality in its highest sense is a progressive discovery of one's will; of the truth that one has a will and can manifest it in the world through other people and other wills. Morality is the reconciling of this will with the ethics to which one chooses to subscribe. And this journey of self-discovery is, in the end, everyone's true life's work. Moreover, for the administrator, the executive, the leader, there is an added charge and a greater responsibility because all organizations and all politics involve the exercise of power over others. If the blind are not to lead the blind, nor the sleeping to lead those who are even deeper asleep, then the leader must have vision, must become more conscious. It is only unfortunate that the maxim which has been with us since the Delphic oracle is so easy to pronounce, so inordinately difficult to accomplish. Nor perhaps should we forget that second command from Delphi: Nothing too much.

Minimaxims

Many, many lists of what might be called adminimaxims, proverbs disparaged by Simon as folk wisdom, have been drawn up over time. No professor of educational administration or public administration or business administration is likely to be without a personal list and particular favorites. Likewise, the leader in the field. Often pithy and succinct, these experiential guides proliferate. What follows is an eclectic selection, consonant with the principles implicit in the main body of this work. I group them under five headings as shown.

(a) Personal

1. Learn from feelings and rebuffs.
2. Don't save stilletos; bury hatchets.
3. Be authentic.
4. Be courteous and well-mannered.
5. Draw a line between private and public life.

The essence here is to avoid, whenever possible, the debilitating effects of negative emotion and to be identified (in the psychological sense) with the role of leader only to the extent dictated by the proper demands of the organization. The leader should be an authentic person with integrity of character. If indeed the leader is to be that, he or she must be more than role and role performance, but must have a private life also. Leaders should realize that their organizations existed before they arrived and will continue after they have gone. No one is indispensable, even though everyone may be irreplaceable.[6] Let the leader seek to be—so far as possible—good and true.

(b) Technique

1. Ask for a proposed solution from problem raisers.
2. Delegate.
3. Remember that Machiavelli has his rightful place.
4. Compartmentalize.
5. Do one's homework.
6. Master parliamentary procedure.
7. Accept that rarely, if ever, is anything simple or complete.

Many more could be added to this list but the above items seem salient and commonsensical. It should also be obvious that, like all maxims, they should be applied judiciously.

(c) Communication

1. Observe channels.
2. Create channels.
3. Empathize.
4. Read.
5. Write.

Leaders who do not read beyond the straightforward (though often burdensome) demands of the job may suffer both by undercutting the third and fourth megamaxims and by diminution of V_4 and V_5 comprehension. Educational leaders especially should be well-read. And may become well-spoken as an advantageous side effect. Reading funds writing and the leader needs to be articulate in the literary sense. Command of language and language games is power, in politics, in life, and in the moral art. Reading and writing coalesce with the imaginative capacity to empathize, to project oneself into another's life, to share emotions and understand motivations. As for channels and media, it goes without saying that these demand untiring oversight and sensitivity.

(d) Timing

1. Delay or retard impulsive reaction.
2. Transact business at the proper place and time.
3. Be punctual and meet deadlines.
4. There is always enough time.

Since administration is an art form that is performed, like music, in the medium of time, it is fitting that time should be mastered and made to serve the leader. Much of time management technique is obvious, elementary, and can be gleaned from a rapid perusal of many business administration or popular texts.[7] What has to be contended with here, however, is psychology rather than logic. The emotional composition of the leader may be such that interruptions and unscheduled contacts, in person or by other means, may be allowed, through the problems they raise, to divert or diffuse the administrator's energy. In this way, an executive's eight-hour day can easily double up to sixteen. One is inclined almost to beware of the over-busy leader in that this very busyness, while it may assuage personal insecurities by giving apparent proof of organizational worth, is itself presumptive evidence of incompetent time management, of superficiality, of being spread too far and too thin. Perhaps the onus should be upon the leader to disprove any such contention. Certainly it should redirect attention, as all timing maxims ultimately do, to the larger maxim of self-observation and self-knowledge.

(e) Work

1. *Nil sine labore.* (Nothing without work)
2. *Labor omnia vincit.* (Work overcomes everything)
3. Work for the work's sake only.

Lastly, some remarks should be made on the topic of attitude to work. It is classic wisdom and not an endorsement of workaholism to say that nothing is accomplished without work and that right work can overcome all obstacles. Work and the expenditure of energy are inescapable in life, but the leader's attitude should be one both of commitment and detachment. Commitment to the work, that it be consistent with the metavalues and the organization purpose. Commitment, that is, at the nomothetic level. This commitment should also be personal, but not to the point of personal identification with task. The moral leader should be indifferent to personal success or failure, detached from the personal consequences of the work as a means to an end, but committed to the work as an end in itself. Such an attitude lifts the leader above the strife. His or her moral integrity then becomes autonomous, independent of the organization, and a source of potential charisma. To work for the work's sake discriminates the artist from the tradesman, the technician from the careerist, the writer from the hack, and the leader from the follower.

At this point, we may now move from practical and specific prescriptions to a more general and abstract summation. In the next section I shall attempt to apply the value paradigm in a prescriptive way to the generality of leadership conceived as a moral and philosophical activity.

General Leadership Prescription

It is possible to summarize all that has been said by applying the value paradigm to the concept of organization and leadership itself. This is done in Table 1.

The central assumption here is that, as we have argued earlier, administration can be conceptually identified with leadership. It then follows that this leadership function permeates the entire organization

TABLE 1

Leadership Value Analysis

Value Type	Value Focus	Hierarchical Level	Philosophical Functional	Curriculum Content
I	Higher Interest and Emotions (Ideals)	Administration	Vision Leadership Policy Charisma Mystique Grand Projects Great Ideas	PPE Psycho-biography Arts Production Dramaturgy Aesthetics Moral Education Protegeship Adventures
IIa	Rational Interests and Emotions	Executive-Managerial (Formal Organization)	Rationality Logic Efficiency Effectiveness Techniques Technology Innovation	Organizational Theory Administrative Theory OR PR Finance and Law Projects Networking Internship Logic Writing Critiquing Economics Political Science
IIb	Social Interests and Emotions	Staff-Technical (Informal Organization)	Organization Morality and Morale Group Processes Teamwork Participation Invention	Group Psychology and Dynamics HR Demystifi-cation Values Education Sabbaticals
III	Lower Interests and Emotions	Rank and File	Discipline Integrity Production Quality Circles Followership	Organizational Culture Rituals Myths Ceremonies Parades Publicity Games-Sports Apprenticeship

from the highest levels of hierarchy, which are most symbolically associated with leadership, to the lowest levels, which are more typically associated with followership. In other words, every member of the organization both has and ought to have some element of leadership responsibility. Even the lowliest member of an organization has the power to commit or not commit himself or herself to the organization's purposes and that, of course, is an administrative and hence a leadership act. This idea is important in educational organizations because there, as we have seen, the lowest level of hierarchy is occupied by the student clientele. From the standpoint of general leadership the students' function, apart from productive learning, is to maintain the organization as an integrated whole by providing it with an enrollment or "student body". This constitutes level III and, as shown in Table 1, corresponds at the individual level of analysis to the value focus of the "body" as the seat of the basic interests and emotions.

In an educational organization, the next level of hierarchy is occupied by the teaching faculty or technical staff, These also constitute the informal organization. Here the leadership function is to maintain social cohesion and a consensus of values which incorporate the "school spirit" or *esprit de corps*. A neglect of this function on the part of the technical staff undermines the motivational climate which is so important in the psychology of learning. This real but abstruse concept, the socio-psychological climate, establishes the V_2 value context or hidden curriculum of the school. It is the nomothetic (V_3) value orientation of the school as interpreted by the teachers. It also influences and sets the standards for performance in the teaching-learning task. A commitment to high standards or excellence is transmitted more through hidden curriculum, teachers' attitudes, and group chemistry than through any formal rhetoric or protestation from higher levels of the organizational hierarchy.

Level IIa is the level of formal organization. The relevant values or metavalues are rationally and logic. At this level, the philosophical function is the implementation of the metavalues and the logical accomplishment of organizational purpose. From the policy maker's standpoint, this is the level at which leadership initiatives are translated into practice. Together with level IIb, it constitutes the planning-politics/mobilizing-managing phase of the administrative cycle discussed above (p. 64).

According to the logic of Table 1 it is at level I that we should find the initiating philosophical drive mechanism, as well as the formal structural leadership, for the organization. At this level is generated the organization's *raison d'e dre*. Note, however, that this level need not exist.

The leadership function of an organization can be merely rational or bureaucratic. That is, it need ascend no higher in the paradigm than level IIa. But if the organization is conceived about a grand project or idea in which there is some element of charismatic commitment or enthusiasm, then it will be characterized as Type I and leadership will then embrace the added functions of vision and mystique as shown. It is conceivable, also, that the charisma and vision of a school's founder may be perpetuated through successive incumbents in the top leadership role.

The analysis also implies that while grand projects and great ideas manifest at level I, it is the function of level II to realize these ideas by means of innovation (structural or otherwise) at IIa and by invention (the development of appropriate curriculum and instruction methodology) at IIb. Ultimately, the test of the great educational idea is whether it captures the allegiance of students; thus, students in effect compose the quality circles that prove or disprove the leadership initiatives.

It is paradoxical that leadership at level III must be termed "followership". Ordinary language is defective in providing us with no other word because the experience of the human race is subliminally conditioned to the leader-follower duality. Even in the technical literature, despite the work of Barnard and many others, the leadership function of rank and file members of the organization goes largely unacknowledged. An exception to this must be made in those instances of Japanese management where the work of quality circles is well-known and in Japanese educational administration, where it is often the case that school norms imbue the lowliest student with a sense of responsibility (and leadership obligation) for the honor and standing of his or her school.

We have thus traced correspondences between the types of value and the philosophical or valuational distribution of the leadership function across the organizational hierarchy. Likewise, the analysis implies a corresponding distribution of emphases if we turn our attention to the matter of leadership training, preparation and development. This is shown in the last column of Table 1.

Leadership Preparation and Development

Structured leader education can be either pre-service or inservice; either outside or inside the organization. At the apex of the paradigm there is the established academic concept of the administrator as a generalist—one whose work is concerned with a level of problem solving and decision making which makes intellectual demands that are best developed through a general knowledge of the human condition rather than through narrow specificities or technical disciplines. This is typified, for example, in the higher reaches of the British Civil Service with its reliance on the Oxonian curriculum of PPE (philosophy, political science, and economics). The paradigm (see Table 1) additionally suggests an intensive and extensive study of such items as psycho-biography, the arts, ethics and aesthetics. For example, Fromm's treatment of Himmler and Gronn's current analysis of the Australian educator Sir James Darling have much to teach us about leadership. Again, actual practice of the arts, such as the writing, staging, production and direction of a film or play, can involve the aspirant leader in the actual doing of leadership with all its attendant human and technical difficulties, and also with some experience of the risk taking involved. Indeed, the lively arts can form a convenient microcosm of administration and a laboratory for leadership. It is only to be wondered that more advantage has not been taken of this obvious connection. Human sensitivity and ruthlessness are simultaneously demanded from the successful director, and all the qualities of leadership are invoked in the translation of an aesthetic idea into its final appearance in the marketplace. Aesthetics, on the other hand, is recommended if only to compensate for the general absence of this sensibility in the world of board rooms, executive offices, and political action. An Oriental instance of this is the tea ceremony, which was conceived not as elite dilettantism or effete aestheticism but as an actual recuperative and inspirational device for the warrior or leader.

The location of moral education at this level goes without saying, if we accept the proposition maintained throughout this book that leadership/administration is a philosophical and moral enterprise. A word needs to be said about protegeship, however. Protegeship is at level I what apprenticeship is at level III. It is an invaluable teaching-learning arrangement. Opportunities for mentoring may not, of course, be always available. The will and the energy for it may be lacking. Moreover, the device is essentially in-service and in-organization and dependent upon imponderable conjunctions of personality, but it should not be overlooked. especially where leader-succession is taken seriously. Of course, protegeship is itself open to corruption, to the possibility of stultifying leadership through dysfunctional executive succession, and this risk, too, should be taken into account.

Finally, at level I, there remains what I have chosen to call adventures. These are projects conceived by the learners themselves in which they put themselves at actual risk in the world. Thus, at the Matsushita School in Japan, students conceive overseas projects by themselves and then go abroad to carry them out. To cite an actual case, a student interested in a political career went to the U.S.A., found employment as an aide to a U.S. congresswoman, and helped her to win her election campaign. He himself is now a successful elected politician in Japan. Adventures such as these are more than conventional projects, in that they require the student to take risks. They must go abroad on their own, find their way in a foreign culture, be prepared for failure as well as success. In short, it is leadership learning by doing, and at the most advanced level.

I shall refrain from commenting at length on the level IIa implications for curriculum because I feel that, in this one domain at least, the preparation of leaders is by and large well provided for at the academic level. The content items listed in the figure are fairly typical of curricula in M.B.A., M.P.A., and M.Ed. or M.A. programs in educational administration. Such preparation can be accomplished either pre- or in-service within the formal academic setting. If such programs fall short, the weakness is likely to be in the areas of logic, writing, and critiquing. These largely philosophical skills are subsumed by the PPE of level I, but, in addition, one has some general sense that our educational managers could profit from training in the ability to perceive logically faulted arguments and from more practice than they receive at present in the art of lucid, concise, and persuasive writing.

If we now continue our analysis at level IIb, we discover that the paradigm here calls for an innovation. This is indicated by the word demystification. The intent here is to suggest that teachers (or technical-professional staff generally) should have at least enough formal training in either administrative or organization theory, or both, to become familiar with the general logic of those disciplines and, thereby, to disabuse themselves of the notion that administration is a mystery or that leaders are of necessity charismatic. (Or for that matter, either fools or knaves.) They should at least be able to understand the difference between the authority deriving from the power of veto and that deriving from the power of expertise. The value logic here is as follows: If we accept the maxim that knowledge is power, then we may further assume that an enhancement of power at this level of hierarchy can become an empowerment, which will encourage and advance leadership at this level.

Technical knowledge in group processes and human relations is also implicitly advocated as stemming from the special philosophical function shown. As for values education, the general point of its merit in understanding organizational duties, responsibilities, obligations and powers is enhanced for educators by the ideological purposes of educational organizations. No educator can be truly that without some special grasp and understanding of the values problem.

I have included sabbaticals at this level because professionals of all kinds, not merely educators, need leave to avail themselves of opportunities for formal and informal learning, to maintain contact with advances in their disciplines, and to refresh and renew their commitment—both to their parent organizations and to their field of expertise. The special applicability to educational organizations derives from the psychological stress factors associated with demanding and multiple daily human interactions. Teaching is a vital pursuit but emotional wear and tear can take an excessive toll.

We now move to consider curriculum content at level III and this brings us forcefully to consider the realities of organizational culture. At this level these are composed of rituals, myths, ceremonies, and the other items shown in Table 1. These aspects of leadership (or followership) curriculum are well known in educational organizations but perhaps not so well understood from the standpoint of value logic. The general intent of such curricular devices is to appeal to and condition the emotions of organization members. An illustration will show how the entire range of paradigmatic values can be incorporated within this sort of cultural manifestation.

An Illustration

Reference has already been made to the Matsushita School of Government and Management. This unique Japanese educational organization has attracted the attention of all the world's leading schools of leadership, such as the *Ecole Normale d'Administration,* the Kennedy School of Government, and the University of Oxford. It has the declared intention of preparing world leaders for the twenty-first century. As a lecturer at that school, I had the privilege of participating in their morning assemblies and it is this ritual I now describe.

At 8:30 a.m. everybody present in the school assembles before a small dais or soapbox and an equally small and casual audio cassette player. Each day a different person, student or staff member, leads the proceedings. The sound of a chime is followed by a minute or so of silence. Then the school song is sung by all. The music, specially commissioned of a famous composer, is sonorous and stately; the words, the product of a noted poet, occasionally inspire student critique but there is no evidence of this now, as all sing with feeling:

> Deep within the earth the red jewel
> is being born;
> One day the earth will shake as
> the volcano erupts....

Then two scrolls are handed to the MC of the day. First he or she recites the following short statement of the school's philosophy:

Having a deep love for our country and our people, searching for guiding philosophy of government and management based on a new concept of man, let us seek to contribute to the prosperity and happiness of mankind, and to the peace of the world.... We firmly dedicate ourselves to the gathering of wisdom; to seeking out the intrinsic nature of reality through independent, self-fulfilling study; and to searching anew each day for the path which will lead us to growth and prosperity.

Then the recitation, with shouted responses, of the five oaths that all members of the school commit themselves to:

1. Carry your original object out to the end
2. Be autonomous and self-reliant
3. Learn from everything
4. Be creative
5. Be grateful and cooperative.

This short ritual is followed by, as it were, orders of the day: general comments on the state of the nation and the school's affairs, notices of visitors, current events and so on. After this the assembly casually breaks up and participants return to work.

The point of this illustration is not to propose any mimicry of this procedure in the West—a mere glance at the wording of the scrolls reveals that the gulf between North America and the Orient is wider than the Pacific Ocean—but to show the application of the paradigm.

The great ideas and the vision associated with the school at level I are dramaturgically and aesthetically conveyed through music, meditation, reverential respect, song, and declamation. The quasi-religious overtones in themselves provide an aspect of moral education. At level II, there are features of networking, group morale, human relations while the functions of communication, efficiency, the metavalues, and even critiquing all have an opportunity of being effected through the commentary and announcements phase. Demystification is likewise operative through the participating presence of the director and executive staff. And finally, of course, the ceremony itself functions directly at level III to maintain discipline, integrity, and commitment of the followership. A member told me that he often questions the merit of his being at the school but that attendance at the assembly always resolves his doubts and re-cements his philosophy.

What does follow from the illustration is confirmation that the value paradigm can provide both descriptive and prescriptive analysis and suggestions for leadership development programs at both in-service and pre-service stages. A deliberate use of this tool in reflective praxis could sophisticate, elaborate, and elevate the moral art of educational leadership.

Educational Administration: A Field for Practical Idealism

I have attempted to show how educational administration is a special case within the general profession of administration. Its leaders find themselves in what might be called an arena of ethical excitement —often politicized but always humane, always intimately connected to the evolution of society, sometimes invested with the Type I values of the culture. Besides, education is both an institution in the sociological sense and a vested interest in the political science sense. It embodies a heritage of value, on the one hand, and is a massive industry on the other, in which social, economic, and political forces are locked together in a complex equilibrium of power. All of this calls for extra-ordinary value sensitivity on the part of educational leaders. And it implies a dialectic of value conflict which it is the leader's duty to manage and which may, at times, feel like a battlefield. In a famous treatise on ethics and morals, J. G. Brennan, after comparing the leader to the protagonist Krishna in the Hindu battlefield epic *Bhagavad Gita*, chooses to close his book with these words:

> Prayer and battle, action and contemplation, what is and what ought to be—each has its own degree of reality, is the lesson of the ancient Hindu scripture. It may be that something of the same doubleness still holds in the realm of ethics and morals. There is the demand of external law, the need of discipline and order, the pressure of the social group that must have its way if the group is to survive. But then there is also the impulse of the individual loving or dissenting heart. Both have their claims, and these claims do not rest on illusion but on *the double nature* of things—on the way things are and on the way things should be. (*my italics*).[8]

We might draw yet another insight from ancient Eastern thought. The dialectic of history dictates three forces: active, passive, and syn-thesizing. Brahman appears metaphysically and figuratively as Crea-tor, Preserver, and Destroyer—constantly dancing the world into ob-livion, recreating it, and maintaining it in its flux. Now education is a very conservative-preservative institution, but if something new is to be born then something old has to make way for it. The educational leader as practical idealist learns to understand these rhythms and seeks, according to personal ideals, to prevent the bad from being born and the good from dying too soon. The leader is not tossed upon the IIb seas by every wave of political opinion, but feels the honor, and the obligations that go with that honor, to participate in an intensely moral vocation. It is not too much to say that, properly conceived, education can be considered as the long sought after "moral equivalent for war." Certainly the conduct of its business and the leadership of its organization should be more than mere pragmatism, positivism, philistinism, and careerism. Whenever educational administration rises above these negatives and becomes what is rightly called leadership, then there is movement from the way things are to the way they ought to be. Then is created the possibility of excellence both for the leader and the led.

Notes

Foreword

1. Jack Culbertson, "Theory in Educational Administration: Echoes from Critical Thinkers," *Educational Researcher* 12, 10 (1983): 15-22.

2. James G. March, ed., *Handbook of Organizations* (Chicago: Rand McNally, 1965), xii.

3. Campbell, R. F., and J. M. Lipham, eds., *Administrative Theory as a Guide to Action,* (Chicago: Midwest Administration Center, University of Chicago, 1960), 24.

4. W. K. Hoy, and C. G. Miskel, *Educational Administration: Theory, Research, and Practice,* 3rd ed. (New York: Random House, 1987), iii.

5. Chirstopher Hodgkinson, *Towards a Philosophy of Administration* (Oxford: Basil Blackwell, 1978), 203, 210, 220, 221.

6. Andrew W. Halpin, "Ways of Knowing", [1960], collected in *Theory and Research in Administration* (New York: MacMillan, 1966), 284.

7. Hodgkinson, *Towards a Philosophy of Administration,* 146.

8. Hodgkinson, *Towards a Philosophy of Administration,* 215.

9. Marcello Craveri, *The Life of Christ,* (New York: Ecco, 1966), 188.

10. March, *Handbook of Organizations,* xi.

Preface

*Every effort has been made in this book to achieve gender-neutral language but, on occasion, the conventional masculine form has been preserved in the interests of clarity, emphasis, or literary merit. It is of course obvious, and acknowledged, that the domain of leadership is one in which the sexes are equally competent.

1. Michael McCrum, *Thomas Arnold, Headmaster,* (Oxford: Oxford University Press, 1989).

Chapter 1

1. T. B. Greenfield, "Organization Theory as Ideology," *Curriculum Inquiry* 9:2 (1979): 207.

2. H. G. Wells, *The Outline of History*, (New York: Doubleday, 1971).

3. Herbert Spencer, *Social Statics*, (London: Williams and Norgate, 1868).

4. Canadian Education Association address by secretary-general. World Organization of Teaching Professions, Toronto, 1984.

5. L. Hay Clyde, *The Blind Spot in American Public Education*, (New York: MacMillan, 1950), 29.

6. C. O. Weber, *Basic Philosophies of Education*, (New York: Rinehart, 1960), 22.

7. John I. Goodlad, *What Schools are For*, (Phi Delta Kappa Educational Foundation, 1979), 123.

8. G. Gentile, *The Reform of Education*, (New York: Harcourt Brace, 1922), 59.

Chapter 2

1. S. Koch, "Review of Learning Theory," address to National Science Foundation, Washington, 1969.

2. Aristotle *The Politics of Aristotle* (London: MacMillan) 1912 orig. *ca.* 330 B.C.

3. A. Hitler, *Mein Kampf*, (New York: Reynal and Hitchcock, 1939).

4. R. F. Campbell, et al. *Introduction to Educational Administration*, 5th ed. (Boston: Allyn and Bacon, 1977), 64.

5. I. Ilich, *Deschooling Society*, (New York: Harper and Row, 1971).

6. G. Hardin, *Exploring New Ethics for Survival*, (New York: Penguin, 1968).

7. Ibid.

8. M. Pastin, *The Hard Problems of Management*, (San Francisco: Jossey-Bass, 1986), 104.

9. T. B. Greenfield, "Organizations as Social Inventions: Rethinking Assumptions About Change," *Journal of Applied Behavioral Science* 9:5 (1973). 551-73.
"The Man Who Comes Back Through the Door in the Wall: Discovering Truth, Discovering Self, Discovering Organizations!" *Educational Administration Quarterly* 6:3 (1980). 26-59.

10. R. Sheldrake, *The New Science of Life,* (Boston: Houghton Mifflin, 1981), 11; J. Monod, *Chance and Necessity,* (London: Fontana, 1974).

11. D. E. Griffiths, "Some Thoughts About Theory in Educational Administration—1975," *UCEA Review* 17:1 (October 1975). 12-18.

12. W. Walker, "Values Unorthodoxy and the 'Unscientific' in Educational Administration Research," *Educational Administration* 6:1 (Winter 1978). 62.

13. R. B. McPherson, R. L. Crowson and N. J. Pitner, *Managing Uncertainty: Administrative Theory and Practice in Education,* (Columbus, OH: Charles E. Merrill, 1986), 19.

14. C. P. Snow, *The Two Cultures and A Second Look,* (New York: Mentor, 1964, 1971).

15. J. W. Getzels, J. M. Lipham and R. F. Campbell, *Educational Administration as a Social Process,* (New York: Harper and Row, 1968), 106.

Chapter 3

1. J. M. Burns, *Leadership,* (New York: Harper and Row, 1978), 2.

2. C. Hodgkinson, *The Philosophy of Leadership,* (Oxford: Blackwell, 1982), 217.

3. L. Wittgenstein, *Tractatus Logico-Philosophicus,* (Oxford: Routledge and Kegan Paul, 1961), 5.6.

4. Ibid., 7.

5. C. Evers, "Hodgkinson on Ethics and the Philosophy of Education," *Educational Administration Quarterly* 21:4 (1985). 27-50. C. Hodgkinson, "Beyond Pragmatism and Positivism," *Educational Administration Quarterly* 22:2 (1986). 5-21.

6. H. A. Simon, *Administrative Behavior,* (New York: Free Press, 1965); Campbell, *Introduction;* McPherson, *Managing Uncertainty.*

7. Chester I. Barnard, *The Functions of the Executive,* (Cambridge, MA: Harvard University Press, 1972).

8. Ibid., xxvii.

9. Hodgkinson, *The Philosophy of Leadership,* 1983, chapter 5.

10. Hodgkinson, ibid., p. 195.

11. M. Weber, A. Henderson and T. Parsons, *The Theory of Social and Economic Organization* (New York: Free Press, 1967).

12. *Time Magazine* (March 23, 1987).

13. Frederick W. Taylor, *The Principles of Scientific Management,* (New York: Harper, 1915); Frederick W. Taylor, *Scientific Management,* (London: Harper, 1964).

14. Hodgkinson, *The Philosophy of Leadership,* 99.

15. e.g. R. K. Merton, *et al., Reader in Bureaucracy* (New York: Free Press, 1952), M. Crozier, *The Bureaucratic Phenomenon,* (Chicago: University of Chicago Press, 1964); A. Downs, *Inside Bureaucracy,* (Boston: 1967); J. D. Thompson, *Organizations in Action,* (New York: McGraw-Hill, 1967); Victor A. Thompson, *Modern Organization,* (New York: Knopf, 1961).

16. e.g. D. B. Tyack, *The One Best System,* (Cambridge, MA: Harvard University Press, 1974); R. Callahan, *Education and the Cult of Efficiency,* (Chicago: University of Chicago Press, 1962); Van Cleve Morris, et al. *Principals in Action: The Reality of Managing Schools,* (Columbus, OH: Charles E. Merrill, 1984); R. F. Campbell, *Introduction;* J. A. Cross in I. Zartmen, ed. *The Negotiation Process,* (Beverly Hills: Sage, 1974); McPherson, *Managing Uncertainty,* 73-76.

17. Hodgkinson, *The Philosophy of Leadership,* 103.

18. Ibid., 106.

19. M. Weber, *The Theory of Social and Economic Organization,* trans. A. Henderson and T. Parsons, (New York: Free Press, 1947), 329-40; Merton.

20. Cf. Victor A. Thompson, *Bureaucracy and the Modern World,* (Morristown, New Jersey: General Learning Press, 1976); Crozier, *The Bureaucratic Phenomenon;* Blau and Scott; A. Etzioni, *Modern Organizations,* (Englewood Cliffs, New Jersey: Prentice-Hall, 1964); Merton.

21. Hodgkinson, *The Philosophy of Leadership,* 151ff.

22. V. Thompson, *Modern Organization.*

23. H. Mintzberg, *The Nature of Managerial Work,* (New York: Harper and Row, 1973).

24. Hodgkinson, *The Philosophy of Leadership,* 156.

25. McPherson, *Managing Uncertainty,* 282.

26. Harry F. Wolcott, *The Main in the Principal's Office,* (New York: Holt, Rinehart and Winston, 1973).

27. T. B. Greenfield, "Organizations as Social Inventions"; T. B. Greenfield, 1979; T. B. Greenfield, "The Man Who Comes Back"; Erving Goffman, *The Presentation of Self in Everyday Life,* (Harmondsworth: Penguin, 1959); Erving Goffman; Edgar H. Schein, *Organizational Culture and Leadership,* (San Francisco: Jossey-Bass, 1985).

28. Thompson, 1961; Goffmann, 1959.

29. Hodgkinson, *The Philosophy of Leadership,* 80ff.

30. H. Zimmer, *Philosophies of India*, (New York: Bollingen Foundation, 1951); Hodgkinson, *The Philosophy of Leadership*, 167-70.

31. W. A. Ouchi, "Markets, Bureaucracies and Class," *Administrative Science Quarterly* (March 1980); P. Drucker, "Behind Japan's Success," *Harvard Business Review* (Jan.-Feb. 1983), 83.

32. A. W. Halpin, *Theory and Research in Administration*, (New York: MacMillan, 1967).

33. Hodgkinson, *The Philosophy of Leadership*, 202.

34. D. L. Stufflebeam, et al. *Educational Evaluation and Decision Making*, (Itasea, IL: Peacock, 1971), 40.

Chapter 4

1. J. W. Getzels and E. Guba, "Social Behavior and the Administrative Process," *School Review* (Winter 1958).

2. Schein, *Organizational Culture*, 5-90.

3. W. H. Whyte, *The Organization Man*, (New York: Simon and Schuster, 1956).

4. Thompson, *Modern Organization*.

5. P. C. Gronn. 1983.

6. T. B. Greenfield, 1980, 1983a.

7. A. Bloom, *The Closing of the American Mind*, (New York: Simon and Schuster, 1987), 172.

8. Taylor, *The Principles of Scientific Management.*

9. F. J. Roethlisberger and W. J. Dickson, *Management and the Worker*, (Cambridge, MA: Harvard University Press, 1939).

10. D. McGregor, *The Human Side of Enterprise*, (New York: McGraw-Hill, 1960), 33-57.

11. Barnard, *The Functions of the Executive*, 153.

12. S. S. Ker and J. Jermier, "Substitutes for Leadership: Their Meaning and Measurement," *Organizational Behavior and Human Performance* 22 (1978), 375-403: S. S. Ker, "Substitutes for Leadership: Some Implications for Organizational Design," *Organization and Administrative Sciences*, 8 (1977), 135-46.

13. Jeans-Jacques Rousseau, *Le Contrat Social*, (Paris, 1762), 11, 7.

14. J. M. Burns, *Leadership*, (New York: Harper and Row, 1978).

15. Campbell, *Introduction*, chapter 2-5.

16. Ibid.

17. Hodgkinson, *The Philosophy of Leadership*, 15, 55.

18. Ibid., 95, 99.

19. Ibid., 30, 168-90.

20. Taylor, *The Principles of Scientific Management*; Callahan, *Education and the Cult of Efficiency*; M. G. Abbott, "Intervening Variables in Organizational Behavior," *Educational Administration Quarterly* (Winter 1965); Campbell, *Introduction*.

21. Sir Geoffrey Vickers, *Human Systems are Different*, (London: Harper and Row, 1983), xxvii.

22. H. Arendt, *Eichmann in Jerusalem*, (New York: Viking, 1963); Vasily Grossman, *Life and Fate*, (London: Collins, 1987); T. Kenneally, *Schindler's List*, (Harmondsworth: Penguin, 1983).

23. Higher education specialists may quibble with this placement but my contention is that these subjects, while having a scientific component, are essentially endeavors about values and hence outside the scientific pale.

24. K. Matsushita, 1988(a).

25. Kurt Lewin, *The Conceptual Representation and Measurement of Psychological Forces*, (Durham, NC: Duke University Press, 1939).

26. J. Dewey, *Representative Selections*, (New York: Library of Liberal Arts, 1966); W. H. Kilpatrick, *Education for a Changing Civilization*, (New York: MacMillan, 1933).

27. Barnard, 1972, 167.

28. Simon, 1965, 116.

29. Bloom, *The Closing of the American Mind*.

30. S. Milgram, *Obedience to Authority*, (New York: Harper and Row, 1974).

31. W. G. Scott and D. K. Hart, *Organizational America*, (Boston:Houghton Mifflin, 1979), 43-46.

32. C. Argyris, *Personality and Organization*, (New York: Harper, 1957), 66.

33. Schein, *Organizational Culture*, 90.

34. T. J. Peters and R. H. Waterman, *In Search of Excellence*, (New York: Harper and Row, 1982).

35. Whyte, *The Organization Man*.

36. S. Cohen and L. Taylor, *Escape Attempts: The Theory and Practice of Resistance to Everyday Life*, (Harmondsworth: Penguin, 1978).

37. Barnard, *The Functions of the Executive*, 23.

38. Burns, *Leadership*, 426, 462.

Chapter 5

1. Mark Holmes, "Comment on 'The Decline and Fall of Science in Educational Administration'," *Interchange* 17:2 (Summer 1986), 85.

2. Hodgkinson, *The Philosophy of Leadership*, 155-56.

3. Immanuel Kant, *Critique of Practical Reason*, (New York: Liberal Arts Press, (1909, 1956), 285.

4. A. J. Ayer, *Language, Truth and Logic*, (London: Gollancz, 1964), 103-10.

5. C. Evers, "Hodgkinson on Ethics"; C. Evers, "Ethics and Educational Administration," *International Encyclopedia of Education*, (Oxford: Pergamon Press, 1989); C. Evers and G. Lakomski, "Knowing Educational Administration: Contemporary Methodological Controversies," in *Educational Administration Research*, (Oxford: Pergamon Press, 1990).

6. M. Nicoll, *Psychological Commentaries on the Teachings of Gurdjieff and Ouspensky*, (London: Shambala, 1984), 469.

7. T. Parsons and E. A. Shils, eds. *Toward a General Theory of Action*, (New York: Harper, 1962), 395.

8. Barnard, *The Functions of the Executive*, 272-78.

9. H. S. Broudy, "Conflicts in Values," in R. E. Ohm and W. Monahan, eds. *Educational Administration: Philosophy in Action*, (Oklahoma City: University of Oklahoma Press, 1965), 42-58.

10. D. Katz and R. Kahn, *The Social Psychology of Organizations*, (New York: Wiley, 1978), 165, 266.

11. Barnard, *The Functions of the Executive*, 159.

Chapter 6

1. Simon, *Administrative Behavior*, 45.

2. Ibid., 45-60, 248-53.

3. Ibid., 249-50.

4. Mintzberg, *The Nature of Managerial Work,* 45, 71-74, 97.

5. Matsushita, 1988(b).

6. R. E. Miles, *Theories of Management,* (New York: McGraw-Hill, 1975), 32-46.

7. Mintzberg, *The Nature of Managerial Work,* 28-29.

8. Max Weber, *The Protestant Ethic and the Spirit of Capitalism,* (New York: Scribner, 1958).

9. Barnard, *The Functions of the Executive,* 203.

10. Simon, *Administrative Behavior,* 29.

11. Thompson, 1961.

12. J. Ladd, "Morality and the Idea of Rationality in Formal Organizations," *The Monist* 4 (1970), 499-500.

13. Barnard, *The Functions of the Executive,* 261.

14. Ibid., 266-67.

15. Plato, *The Republic,* (Harmondsworth: Penguin, 1975), 288.

16. Swami Vividishananda, *A Man of God,* (Madras: Sri Ramakrishna Math, 1957), 188.

17. Barnard, *The Functions of the Executive,* 282.

18. Daniel L. Duke, "Why Principals Consider Quitting," *Phi Delta Kappan* 70:4 (December 1988), 308.

19. Greenfield, 1983(b).

20. Matsushita, 1988(b), 310.

Chapter 7

1. Hodgkinson, *The Philosophy of Leadership,* 202, 1.1.

2. Broudy, "Conflicts in Values," 42-58.

3. Hodgkinson, 1983, 34.

4. Ibid., 197.

5. Simon, *Administrative Behavior.*

6. Hodgkinson, 1983, 111.

7. Bossert, et al. "The Instructional Management Role of the Principal," *Educational Administration Quarterly* 18 (Summer 1982), 34; McPherson, et al. *Managing Uncertainty,* 52.

8. J. G. Brennan, *Ethics and Morals,* (New York: Harper and Row, 1978), 350.

References

Abbott, M. G. "Intervening Variables in Organizational Behaviour." *Educational Administration Quarterly*. Winter 1965.

Arendt, N. *Eichmann in Jerusalem*. New York: Viking, 1963.

Argyris, C. *Personality and Organization*. New York: Harper, 1957.

Ayer, A. J. *Language, Truth and Logic*. London: Gollancz, 1964.

Barnard, C. *The Functions of the Executive*. Cambridge, MA: Harvard University Press, 1972.

Blau, P. M. *The Dynamics of Bureaucracy*. Chicago: University of Chicago Press, 1955.

Blau, P. M. and W. R. Scott, *Formal Organizations*. San Francisco: Chandler, 1962.

Bloom, A. *The Closing of the American Mind*. New York: Simon & Schuster 1987.

Bossert, et al. "The Instructional Management Role of the Principal." *Educational Administration Quarterly* 18 (Summer 1982).

Brennan, J. G. *Ethics and Morals*. New York: Harper and Row, 1973.

Broudy, H. S. "Conflicts in Values" in R. E. Ohm, and W. Monahan, eds. *Educational Administration: Philosophy in Action*. Tulsa: University of Oklahoma, 1965.

Burns, J. M. *Leadership*. New York: Harper and Row, 1978.

Callahan, R. *Education and the Cult of Efficiency*. Chicago: University of Chicago Press, 1962.

Campbell, R. F. et al. *Introduction to Educational Administration* 5th ed. Boston: Allyn & Bacon, 1977 (1987).

Canadian Education Association address by Secretary-General. *World Organization of Teaching Professions*. Toronto, 1984.

Clyde, L. Hay *The Blind Spot in American Public Education*. New York: MacMillan, 1950.

Cohen, S., and L. Taylor *Escape Attempts: The Theory and Practice of Resistance to Everyday Life*. Harmondsworth: Pelican, 1978.

Cross, J. A. in I. Zartman ed. *The Negotiation Process*. Beverly Hills: Sage, 1974.

Crozier, M. *The Bureaucratic Phenomenon*. Chicago: University of Chicago Press, 1964.

Dewey, J. *Representative Selections*. New York: Library of Liberal Arts, 1966.

Downs, A. *Inside Bureaucracy*. Boston: Little Brown, 1967.

Drucker, P. "Behind Japan's Success." *Harvard Business Review* 83 (January-February 1981).

Duke, Daniel L. "Why Principals Consider Quitting." *Phi Delta Kappan* 70:4 (December 1988).

_____ . *School Leadership and Instruction Improvement*. New York: Random House, 1987.

Etzioni, A. *Modern Organizations*. Englewood Cliffs, NJ: Prentice-Hall, 1964.

Evers, C. "Hodgkinson on Ethics and the Philosophy of Adminstration." *Educational Administration Quarterly* 21:4 (1985):27-50.

_____ . *"Ethics and Educational Administration"* International Encyclopedia of Education. Oxford: Pergamon Press, 1989,

_____ . and G. Lakomski "Knowing Educational Administration:Contemporary Methodological Controversies" in *Educational Administration Research*. Oxford: Pergamon Press, 1990.

Gentile, G. *The Reform of Education*. New York: Harcourt, Brace. 1922.

Getzels, J. W. and E. Guba "Social Behaviour and the Administrative Process." *School Review* Winter 1958.

Getzels, J. W., J. M. Lipham and R. F. Campbell *Educational Administration as a Social Process*. New York: Harper and Row, 1968.

Goffmann, Erving *The Presentation of Self in Everyday Life*. Harmondsworth: Penguin, 1959.

_____ . *Asylums*. Garden City, NY: Doubleday, 1961.

Goodlad, John I. *What Schools are For*. Phi Delta Kappa Educational Foundation, 1979.

Greenfield, T. B. "Organizations as Social Inventions: Rethinking Assumptions About Change." *Journal of Applied Behavioral Science* 9:5(1973):551-73.

_____ . Theory About Organization: A New Perspective and Its Implications for School" in M. G. Hughes, *Administering Education: International Challenge*. London: Athlone, 1975, 71-99.

————. "Organization Theory as Ideology." *Curriculum Inquiry* 9:2 (1979): 97-112.

————. "Research in Educational Administration in the United States and Canada: An Overview and Critique," *Educational Administration 8:1 (1979-80):207-45.*

————. "The Man Who Comes Back Through the Door in the Wall: Discovering Truth, Discovering Self, Discovering Organizations!" *Educational Administration Quarterly* 16:3(1980):26-59.

————. "Against Group Mind: An Anarchistic Theory of Organization" in *Reflective Readings in Educational Administration.* Victoria, Australia: Deakin University 1983a, 293-301.

————. "Environment as Subjective Reality." Manuscript, 1983b.

Griffiths, D. E. "Some Thoughts about Theory in Educational Administration -1975." *UCEA Review.* 17:1 (October 1975).

Gronn, P. C. "Talk as the Work: The Accomplishment of School Administration." *Administrative Science Quarterly 28(1) 1983:1-21.*

————. "The Boyhood, Schooling and Early Career of J. R. Darling, 1899-1930." *Journal of Australian Studies. 19 (1986):30-42.*

Grossman, Vasily. *Life and Fate.* London: Collins, 1987.

Halpin, A. W. *Theory and Research in Administration.* New York: MacMillan, 1967.

Hardin, G. *Exploring New Ethics for Survival.* New York: Penguin, 1968.

Hitler, A. *Mein Kampf.* New York: Reynal & Hitchcock, 1939.

Hodgkinson, C. *Towards a Philosophy of Administration.* Oxford: Blackwell, 1978.

————. *The Philosophy of Leadership.* Oxford: Blackwell, 1982, 1983.

————. "Beyond Pragmatism and Positivism." *Educational Administration Quarterly* 22:2 (1986):5-21.

Holmes, Mark. "Comment on 'The Decline and Fall of Science in Educational Administration'." *Interchange* 17:2 (Summer 1986):80-90.

Ilich, I. *Deschooling Society* New York: Harper and Row, 1971.

Kant, Immanuel. *Critique of Practical Reason.* New York: Liberal Arts Press, (1909), 1956.

Katz, D. and R. Kahn, *The Social Psychology of Organizations.* New York: Wiley, 1978.

Kenneally, T. *Schindler's List.* Harmondsworth: Penguin, 1983.

Ker, S. S. "Substitutes for Leadership: Some Implications for Organizational Design." *Organization and Administrative Sciences* 8 (1977):135-146.

_____ . and J. Jermier "Substitutes for Leadership: Their Meaning and Measurement." *Organizational Behavior and Human Performance* 22 (1978) :375-403.

Kilpatrick, W. H. *Education for a Changing Civilization.* New York: MacMillan, 1933.

Koch, S. "Review of Learning Theory" address to *National Science Foundation.* Washington, 1969.

Ladd, J. "Morality and the Ideal of Rationality in Formal Organizations" *The Monist* 54 (1970):688.

Lewin, K. *The Conceptual Representation and Measurement of Psychological Forces.* Durham, NC: Duke University Press, 1939.

Matsushita, K. *Not for Bread Alone. A Business Ethos, A Management Ethic.* Osaka: PHP Institute, 1988(a).

_____ . *Portrait of an Industrialist.* Osaka: PHP Institute, 1988(b).

McCrum, Michael. *Thomas Arnold, Headmaster.* Oxford: Oxford University Press, 1989.

McGregor, D. *The Human Side of Enterprise.* New York: McGraw-Hill, 1960.

McPherson, R. B., R. L. Crowson, and N. J. Pitner, *Managing Uncertainty: Administrative Theory and Practice in Education.* Columbus, OH: Charles E. Merrill, 1986.

Merton, R. K. et al. *Reader in Bureaucracy* New York: Free Press, 1952.

Miles, R. E. *Theories of Management.* New York: McGraw-Hill, 1975.

Milgram, S. *Obedience to Authority.* New York: Harper and Row, 1974.

Mintzberg, H. *The Nature of Managerial Work.* New York: Harper and Row, 1973.

Monod, J. *Chance and Necessity.* London: Fontana, 1974.

Morris, Van Cleve et al. *Principals in Action: The Reality of Managing School.* Columbus, OH: Charles E. Merrill, 1984.

Nicoll, M. *Psychological Commentaries on the Teachings of Gurdjieff and Ouspensky.* London: Shambala, 1984.

Ouchi, W. A. "Markets, Bureaucracies, and Class." *Administrative Science Quarterly* (March 1980).

Parsons, T. and E. A. Shils, eds. *Toward a General Theory of Action.* New York: Harper, 1962.

Pastin, M. *The Hard Problems of Management.* San Francisco: Jossey-Bass, 1986.

Peters, T. J. and R. H. Waterman, *In Search of Excellence.* New York: Harper and Row, 1982.

Plato. *The Republic.* Harmondsworth: Penguin, 1975.

Roethlisberger, F. J. and W. J. Dickson, *Management and the Worker.* Cambridge, MA: Harvard University Press, 1939.

Rousseau, Jean-Jacques. *Le Contrat Social.* Paris, 1762.

Schein, Edgar H. *Organizational Culture and Leadership.* San Francisco: Jossey-Bass, 1985.

Scott, Wm. G. and D. K. Hart, *Organizational America.* Boston: Houghton Miflin, 1979.

Sheldrake, R. *The New Science of Life.* Boston: Houghton Mifflin, 1981.

Simon, H. A. *Administrative Behavior.* New York: Free Press, 1965.

Snow, C. P. *The Two Cultures and a Second Look.* New York: Mentor, 1964, 1971.

Spencer, Herbert. *Social Statics,* London: Williams and Norgate, 1868.

Stufflebeam, D. L. et al. *Educational Evaluation and Decision Making.* Itasea, IL: Peacock, 1971.

Taylor, F. W. *The Principles of Scientific Management.* New York: Harper, 1915.

_____ . *Scientific Management.* London: Harper, 1964.

Thompson, J. D. *Organizations in Action.* New York: McGraw-Hill, 1967.

Thompson, V. *Modern Organization.* New York: Knopf, 1961.

_____ . *Bureaucracy and the Modern World.* Morristown, NJ: General Learning Press, 1976.

Tyack, D. B. *The One Best System.* Cambridge, MA: Harvard University Press, 1974.

Vickers, Sir Geoffrey. *Human Systems are Different.* London: Harper and Row, 1983.

Vividishananda, Swami. *A Man of God.* Madras: Sri Ramakrishna Math, 1957.

Walker, W. "Values, Unorthodoxy, and the 'Unscientific' in Educational Administration Research." *Educational Administration* 6:1 (Winter 1978).

Weber, C. O. *Basic Philosophies of Education.* New York: Rinehart, 1960.

Weber, M. tr. A. Henderson and T. Parsons, *The Theory of Social and Economic Organization.* New York: Free Press, 1947.

_____ . *The Protestant Ethic and the Spirit of Capitalism* (1930). New York: Scribner, 1958.

Wells, E. G. *The Outline of History*, Chapter 15. New York: Doubleday, 1971.

Whyte, W. H. *The Organization Man*. New York: Simon and Schuster, 1956.

Wittgenstein, L. *Tractatus Logico-Philosophicus*. Oxford: Routledge and Kegan Paul, 1961.

Wolcott, Harry F. *The Man in the Principal's Office*. New York: Holt, Rinehart and Winston, 1973.

Zimmer, H. *Philosophies of India*. New York: Bollingen Foundation, 1951.

Index